Richard Denis Shaw, PhD

Chaplains to the Imprisoned:

Sharing Life with the Incarcerated

Pre-publication
REVIEW

"**C**haplains to the Imprisoned explores the world of the most long-standing but least understood of prison workers. Shaw knows his subject well. His work is a powerful amalgam of personal experience, exhaustive historical study, and sophisticated survey research. His extensive career in prison and jail chaplaincy informs the analysis, but Shaw lets his colleagues speak–about the challenges and stresses, rewards and pains, frustrations and victories in ministering to society's outcasts. He does a masterful job of telling their stories, and shows chaplains to be empathic, committed, optimistic, and pragmatic. As Shaw demonstrates, 'there is a quiet sense of the heroic in what these men and women accomplish out of love for God and humanity.'

This is a first-rate scholarly work on prison and jail chaplaincy that should be read by anyone interested in prisons and prison reform–correctional administrators and managers, law makers, community leaders, and volunteers. Religious leaders will gain important insights into this demanding ministry through Shaw's book, and a better appreciation of chaplains' need for support from congregations and religious organizations in carrying out their work."

Timothy J. Flanagan, PhD
Professor and Dean,
College of Criminal Justice,
Sam Houston State University

CHAPLAINS TO THE IMPRISONED

SHARING LIFE WITH THE INCARCERATED

HAWORTH Criminal Justice, Forensic Behavioral Sciences & Offender Rehabilitation

Nathaniel J. Pallone, PhD
Senior Editor

New, Recent, and Forthcoming Titles:

Treating Sex Offenders in Correctional Institutions and Outpatient Clinics: A Guide to Clinical Practice by William E. Prendergast

The Merry-Go-Round of Sexual Abuse: Identifying and Treating Survivors by William E. Prendergast

Chaplains to the Imprisoned: Sharing Life with the Incarcerated by Richard Denis Shaw

Forensic Neuropsychology: Conceptual Foundations and Clinical Practice by Jose A. Valciukas

CHAPLAINS TO THE IMPRISONED

SHARING LIFE WITH THE INCARCERATED

RICHARD DENIS SHAW
Siena College & Albany County Correctional Facility

THE HAWORTH PRESS, INC.
New York – London – Norwood (Australia)

The Haworth Press, Inc., 10 Alice Street, Binghamton, NY 13904-1580

Library of Congress Cataloging-in-Publication Data

Shaw, Richard Denis.
    Chaplains to the imprisoned : sharing life with the incarcerated / Richard Denis Shaw
       p.   cm.
    Includes bibliographical references and index.
    ISBN 1-56024-877-7
    1. Chaplains, Prison–New York. 2. Prisons–New York–Officials and employees. 3. New York (State)–Officials and employees.
    I. Title.
BV4340.S485 1994
259'.5'09747–dc20
                                                  94-26530
                                                     CIP

ABOUT THE AUTHOR

Richard Denis Shaw, a native of Brooklyn, was ordained to the priesthood in the Roman Catholic Church in 1968. In his quarter century of ministry, he has served as a jail and prison chaplain for 21 years. He has also taught on the high school and college levels, most recently at Maria College in Albany and at Siena College in Loudonville, New York, with which he is presently affiliated. In addition to his chaplaincy at the Albany County Reformatory, he ministers to a small county parish, St. John Francis Regis, in Grafton, New York. Father Shaw received his PhD in criminal justice from the State University of New York at Albany.

Father Shaw is the author of a novel entitled *The Christmas Mary Had Twins* and of two volumes of biography: *Dagger John*, about Archbishop John Hughes of New York, and *John Dubois: Founding Father*.

Contents

Chapter 1

PROLOGUE: QUEST FOR IDENTITY IN THE CHAPLAINCY

FROM PERSONAL TO EMPIRICAL

Like many men and women who serve as chaplains to the incarcerated, I found myself in this ministry without any prior ambition for the role or knowledge of what the ministry involved. In 1972, while studying in Boston, I responded to a call to assist the chaplain at that city's Charles Street Jail. A year later, upon returning to my home in the Capital District of New York State, I assumed the chaplaincy of Rensselaer County Jail, gradually adding the facilities of Schenectady and Albany Counties to what friends began to refer to as my "empire of jails."

In the late 1980s, intrigued by the idea of Shock Incarceration, I took on the chaplaincy at a New York State prison geared toward this "boot camp" approach to dealing with young, first time felony offenders. After the first decade of working in the field I decided to go back to school in part "to see what the theorists are saying." The pursuit of a doctorate in Criminal Justice revealed to me that the theorists knew (or perhaps cared) almost nothing about chaplains and chaplaincy, despite the fact that in most facilities in this country, chaplains are the only personnel, other than Corrections Officers, who regularly interact with inmates on the tier areas. Medical personnel, psychologists, social workers, and other clinical personnel call inmates from tier areas for consultation. Chaplains see them where they live and interact with other inmates. This alone gives chaplains a perspective which would make them a valid and interesting subject for study.

And yet, the literature in the field is all but naked of references to them. In one rare study (an unpublished 1956 dissertation on the social roles of chaplains of differing Faith groups), author George

Murphy observed that although "prison communities have been an object of study for a number of years . . . Criminologists generally have given very little energy to religion. Most have simply ignored the fact of religion and some have been openly antagonistic" (1956:6).

Religious thinkers had great influence in the birth of the prison system in the United States, as elsewhere in the world. Ironically, however, when religious ministers attempted to enter these facilities to minister to inmates, they usually found themselves regarded as strangers and aliens in this system created by religous impetus. Not only has their role been misunderstood, rarely has been found even so much as a clearly defined, universally accepted idea of what chaplains were to be and do in penal institutions.

During each era of constantly changing philosophies of penology in this country, chaplains have had to fight for every inch of turf gained, establishing their role in each separate facility in which they worked, as if each one of them had to re-invent what chaplaincy was. Definitions of what a chaplain should be, either when put forth by themselves or others, were subjective and applied to local situations. These were rarely nurtured by general usage and time into any concepts which might be considered as objective and universal in scope.

Initiating my own quest for a portrait of chaplaincy with a search through the literature of the field of criminal justice, I found that references to chaplains were often so peripheral and passing in nature that they were not included in the indices of books. Like panning for nuggets one had to sift through each and every prison book hoping that the chaplain would make a momentary appearance on one of its pages. The process was worth the effort, and the nuggets which will be shared in the first section of this study were often pure gold; sometimes damning, sometimes praising those chaplains who made such momentary appearances.

Chaplains are, indeed, controversial figures. The value of their presence within jails and prisons has never been wholly agreed upon by other personnel working within facilities, by inmates, by observers of the criminal justice system, or even by other members of the clergy. Nonetheless, their presence cannot by ignored, and their importance can well be measured by Daniel Glaser's discovery about their impact. In his classic study *The Effectiveness of a Prison and Parole System*, he noted that chaplains "constitute only a fraction of the total prison staff" within the system (1964:145). But their impact upon inmates and upon the system itself was then measured alongside the impact of those within facilities who, by far, outnumber them. Glaser found that one-sixth of those inmates in his study who were successful after their release said that the chaplains at their facilities had been a major influence in their reformation. Such a realization should make chaplaincy worthy of greater attention than has been given to it.

SOLICITING THE INPUT OF OTHER CHAPLAINS

After allowing observers to portray chaplains in the first part of this study, I then wanted chaplains to be able to portray themselves. I reasoned that it was advantageous that the gathering and editing of such a self-portrait be done by someone who is both a member of the clergy and a chaplain with a generation's time of work experience within jail and prison facilities. Many writers approach any topic concerning the clergy either with trepidation, treating them as sacrosanct, or, at the other extreme, often making sweeping generalizations which have the ring of iconoclasm. Both extremes, and even moderate approaches, tend to present the clergy as if they were somehow not quite human.

This writer who, as a clergyperson, is already beyond this barrier, accepts as a matter of fact the human qualities (failings as well as virtues) in himself and others who serve in ministry. Unlike Corrections Officers who work every day with a large peer group, chaplains work in near isolated circumstances. The pooling of shared experiences and opinions can be a means of reducing this day-to-day sense of isolation. In this instance, chaplains would be responding to a peer and an insider to their world. Such an element of commonality, it was hoped, would produce a sense of confidence and encourage them to be open and frank about sharing what they perceive to be concerns within their ministry.

Having spent many evenings, both at formal conventions and at private gatherings, listening to chaplains regale one another with stories and comparisons of their respective fields of ministry, I formulated a questionnaire, borne of such discussions, and then ran it by individual chaplains until it was welded into what seemed to be a good instrument for self-portrait.

The men and women whose input was solicited felt that more should be requested of the chaplains than a self-portrait. Chaplains can become nearly as street smart as the people they serve. If they are going to take time to fill out a questionnaire it would have to serve some practical purpose. My colleagues felt that the daily difficulties, problematic issues and stressful factors which chaplains share in such a ministry should be measured and presented. These should, then, be balanced alongside the experiental wisdom of individual chaplains who would make suggestions as to how chaplains might change, alleviate or learn to cope with such difficulties, issues, and stressful factors.

CHAPLAINCY AND STRESS

Few people would contest that chaplaincy within jails and prisons is a tough ministry. That this is accepted as "a given" was borne home to me several years ago when we were having a particularly rough time at the Albany facility. During a heat wave which frayed already bad tempers into near riot situations the inmates on the second east tier attempted to take an officer hostage during their time in the yard.

Not only was that tier put in 24 hour lock-in, so too was the third east tier which had fomented much of the trouble from windows facing the yard. For security purposes both tiers were forbidden to go to communal religious services that weekend. The administration asked the chaplains to go to each cell, bringing services to those on the tiers who wanted to pray.

On a day-to-day basis, we Christian ministers work well as a team: two Baptists, an Episcopalian and myself as Roman Catholic. We went to the cell blocks together and as we moved along the tiers we encountered the full fury of all the anger which had built up. We were cursed, vilified, and spit at.

As soon as we were out in the main hallway, one of the two Baptist ministers, Rev. Cleveland Everette, visibly shaken, mopped from his brow the perspiration (and whatever else had landed there), sighed, and murmured: "There's got to be an easier way to make a living."

The evening after this occurrence, I was standing in the rectory kitchen talking with the two parish priests with whom I lived at St. Pius Xth Church in nearby Loudonville. The telephone rang, and the young associate pastor answered it. As I learned afterwards, an angry voice at the other end yelled at him: "I'm gonna kill you, Mothah F — kah!"

Without answering a word, he blanched and handed the receiver to me: "It's for you," he said. It was not the head of the Rosary Altar Society, and, yes, he was right; it was for me. If it is thus accepted that some of the demands of chaplaincy go beyond the expected rigors of day-to-day parish ministry, these stressful factors, and the wear and tear they imply, should be examined in any full portrait of chaplains.

The use of the word "stress," pioneered and popularized by the distinguished psychoanalyst Hans Selye (1956), has snowballed in the clinical literature into a catch-all term which is simultaneously applied to the subject studied, the environment in which the subject exists, and to the transaction between the subject and the environment. In recent years a great number of articles and books have been written which focus upon a type of career related stress labeled "burn out." Many of these works have chosen, as subjects, people who work in service oriented occupations and much of what is said in these studies about the problems of persons in helping professions would seem applicable to the clergy in penal institutions. H. J. Freudenberger, the father of the "burnout" concept, notes that "the helping professions get to see a lot of failure and misery." These professions attract "determined idealists" who are "dynamic, charismatic goal oriented men and women." In the face of constant discouragement they learn to wear a facade of optimism and encouragement and this takes its toll. "When trouble sets in," Freudenberger and Richelson observe, "it is usually a result of overcommitment or overdedication." They add, "Whenever the expectation level is dramatically opposed to reality and the person persists in trying to reach that expectation, trouble is on the way" (1980:13, 45).

The personality factors of subjects introduce a subjective element into any study of stress. As observed by Veninga and Spradley: "each person learns to see the world through stress-colored glasses . . . But the character of the lens differs for each of us so that an event that brings intense, unrelieved stress for one individual may affect another in only a minor way" (1981:29). In this respect, one must keep in mind that the subjects of this study are people sensitive enough to have dedicated their lives to God's purposes. Spiritual writers speak of the idea of "kenosis," that the person of God is one whose life is poured out for others. As beautiful as this idea is, such a manner of living is not accomplished without cost and pain. Louis Camelli, in a remarkable article entitled "The Response of Spirituality," notes that "ministry does not engage a person merely on the level of task . . . it engages the whole person," and that "some stress in ministry results in a displaced sense of responsibility" (1979:105).

Christina Maslach has explored sources of burnout among diverse members of helping professions. "Obviously," she notes, "it is more pleasant and personally rewarding to be involved with someone who is likeable than with someone who is a pain in the neck." The prison chaplain reaches out to embrace very many people who might fit into the latter category. Referring to the sense of overload which this creates, Maslach makes an example of the scene in *Jesus Christ Superstar* in which Christ, swamped with people who want his help, wearily says: "You're pressing — too closely. There are too many of you and too little of me" (1981:23, 40).

Strictly speaking many studies of stress are most concerned with inappropriate responses stress situations. Given this insider's vantage point of having observed as many chaplains as I have over many years of time, it was presumed that this study would find chaplains working in situations which are unpleasant and harsh but which are within the boundaries of their capabilities for coping. In this respect, we are mostly dealing with nondisabling stress stimuli, and that this fact would color the responses made in a self-report study. However, reports of disequilibrating, unsettling, disquieting, annoying but managable stressors are nonetheless valuable for the sake of identifying job-related difficulties which routinely affect performance and which might be reduced as threats or impediments or hurdles.

The questionnaire which was sent to chaplains (included in the Appendices) asked each to describe his/her ministry. Following this, a double, five-point Likert Scale was used for 29 factors which might affect one's ministry within a facility and which might be labeled as problematic or stress-inducing. Each of these could be rated by the chaplains as to the frequency with which the conditions were encountered (ranging from "never" to "occasional" to "constant") and the intensity of their experienced demand (ranging form "not at all" to "moderate" to "significant").

The observations matched against these scales were divided into two-item groups. The first grouping focused upon stress brought about by conditions created by the nature of the facility. The second grouping focused upon one's relationships with other people while working as a chaplain. Both sets of observations were followed by open-ended questions which asked the respondent to point to situations different from those cited which he/she might regard as pertinent to the subject, even though they had not been touched upon in the questionnaire.

The first group of observations (those focusing upon stress factors associated with the nature of the facility) included:

- Physical danger
- Fears of contracting an illness such as AIDS
- Noise factors
- The invasion of inmates' privacy
- Preaching of love in a punishment setting
- Overcrowding and work overload
- Disruptions at religious services
- Working for both Church and State
- Dealing with bureaucracy
- Fitting in facility scheduling
- Injustices within the system and within the facility
- Working in a dead end ministry
- Seeing little results from one's work
- Isolation from other clergy

The second group of observations, dealing with relationships, included:

- Backsliding of rehabilitated inmates
- Infrequency of success stories
- Being used by con artists
- The social chasm between chaplains and inmates
- The monotony of inmate woes
- Dealing with the personal tragedies of inmates
- Inmate suicide
- Dealing with emotional feeling about inmates
- Dealing with the amorality of inmates
- Coping with dislikeable inmates

- Coping with mentally ill inmates
- Dealing with confidentiality
- Racial and religious tensions
- Becoming jaded
- Representing the system
- Friction with other staff members and clergy

The questionnaire concluded with further open-ended questions wherein the respondent was asked to contribute ideas for strategies that might be helpful in coping with stress-related conditions. The subjects of these questions included:

- What advice should be given to new chaplains
- How one should evaluate one's own contributions as a chaplain
- Any specific techniques the respondent had found effective in coping with ministry-related stress
- Where chaplains might turn for professional and emotional support
- How the respondent's philosophy of jail/prison ministry has changed through the years, owing to experiences in chaplaincy work.

The questionnaire ended with a request for added perspective or understanding which the contributor had evolved based upon his or her experience as a chaplain.

ADVENTURES IN THE FIELDS OF RESEARCH

The questionnaire was mailed to every Protestant, Catholic, Jewish and Islamic chaplain listed as an official chaplain in the Federal and State prison systems within New York State. The questionnaires, with a stamped, addressed envelope for return, were mailed to the chaplains at the prison facilities, each chaplain being addressed individually rather than having the survey sent to them as a group through the chaplain's offices. A total of 156 questionnaires was sent out in the State system. The process of getting the questionnaire into the hands of chaplains was an adventure in itself, one which gave evidence of the obscure position of chaplains within the system. One problem with the list of chaplains sent to me by the State Department of Corrections was that no clergy titles (e.g., Reverend, Father, Rabbi, Imam) preceded the names. When I asked for these, I was told that the Department did not keep a record of chaplains by denomination; that they were simply listed as "chaplains."

Now, since I was one of the Department's employees and because they very well knew that I served as a Catholic priest and supervised me as such with regard my responsibilities to them, I knew that this was not the case — and said so. A politely insistent bureaucrat assured me that the Department had no list of its chaplains by denomination. A number of phone calls to various personnel in Albany's central offices kept providing me with the same mis- or non-information. At length, I stopped beating my head against this stone wall and added a handwritten note to each cover letter accompanying the questionnaire, apologizing to each recipient for my generic and impersonal form of address to him/her merely as "Chaplain —." I regretted this lack for it made the letter seem less personal. This waltz with central offices turned out to be prescient of the frequently volatile responses I would receive from chaplains about their own dealings with administrative personnel.

Nine questionnaires were sent to chaplains serving in the Federal system in New York State, this limited list of names having been provided by the chief chaplain of the Federal Bureau of Prisons in Washington, D.C., following a request to send the questionnaire to the chaplains in their entire system. The survey instrument was also sent to the chaplains of each county and city jail in New York State with a capacity of 500 or more inmates. In small county jails, the role of chaplain is often undertaken as an aside to duties pertaining to a congregation. Such chaplains were excluded because this study focuses upon clergy for whom jail chaplaincy is a major part of his/her ministry. The dividing point of 500 inmates is arbitrary, but it would seem reasonable to suppose that a facility of this minimum size or larger would require a substantial commitment of time in one's ministerial schedule.

Aside from a list provided by the Riker's Island complex of jail facilities, there was no obtainable list of chaplains' names for county jails in New York State. However, the New York State Sheriff's Association agreed to include an informational notice about the questionnaire in their routine mailing sent to sheriff's departments throughout the state. The questionnaires were sent to each facility addressed to the chaplains individually by denomination (e.g., "Protestant Chaplain"). Fifty-three questionnaires were sent to chaplains of jails.

POLITICAL FACTORS AFFECTING SURVEY RETURN

The antagonism toward, or, perhaps better, the indifferent belittlement of chaplaincy was exemplified by a political incident which coincided with this present study. The mailing of the questionnaire throughout the state accidentally took place in the same week (to my chagrin) that a widely publicized proposal was made that chaplains might easily be eliminated from the prison system for the sake of trimming New York State's perennially overloaded budget. The threat of the cut came from the office of Thomas Coughlin, Commissioner of Correctional Services. Alan Davitt of the New York State Catholic Conference explained the motivation for the proposed cut to this writer, saying that it was no more than a move to save money. Chaplaincy was vulnerable in such a situation, Davitt explained, because in the paradigm of administrative thought, "chaplaincy doesn't fit a programs model." That chaplaincy does not fit into a programs model is not without the state attempting to make it do so. Chaplains ministering in prisons and jails must funnel their ministry through the secular procedures of the facility, oftentimes pleasing program directors by filling out seemingly endless triplicate forms which have nothing to do at all with his or her real work with inmates.

In the final analysis, the work of the chaplain, usually done in a setting of confidentiality, is beyond secular description and unmeasurable by any bureaucratic standards. The bureaucratic frustration in dealing with an employee whose role is non-measurable was reinforced to this writer by a conversation with the New York State Department of Corrections' Director of Family and Ministerial Services, who expressed a strong opinion that working with chaplains is not easy, that many of the chaplains are not pulling their own weight, and that some chaplains blatantly refuse to fit into the system. Since the administrator was speaking with a Catholic he expressed added bewilderment that this should be so of Catholic priests, since the Catholic Church itself is so heavily structured. He failed to perceive that, although state and Church are both tightly structured, the work product for each does not share the same criteria for evaluation. The least-busy clergyperson by external appearances could be the most productive in ministering to people and vice versa. The "product" is simply beyond measurement from a program-oriented perspective. After the budget cut was publicized in the media, representatives of all the major faith groups joined together in opposition to it.

When, as Davitt related, the Commissioner insisted that the cut was a "fait accompli" the religious lobby approached state legislators for relief. Legislators, according to Davitt, may ignore religious groups when they take a stand about a controversial public issue (such as the death penalty), but when they unite about an issue in which religious groups per se are affected, politicians, with an eye to voters back home, generally bow to them. Unsurprisingly, therefore, the chaplaincy item was restored when the budget was revised.

Even if the proposed axing of chaplaincy had gone through, the Department of Corrections would only have had to reintroduce chaplaincy to get out of the no-win situation it would have created. According to minimum standards which are clearly spelled out in law, inmates cannot be denied the exercise of their religion. By having on deck official clergy representing the major faith groups, administrators of facilities fulfill this requirement of law, and can refuse entry to religious zealots constantly showing up at prisons, wishing to gain entry to "save souls." Do away with chaplains, and administrators would have to deal, on a case-by-case basis, with every inmate's personally chosen "spiritual director." Even with so mainline a religion as Roman Catholicism, this would mean that each inmate could claim his/her right to have weekly mass celebrated for him/her by any individual priest willing to show up. The only way to do away with this potential administrative nightmare would be to change the State's laws regarding minimum standards and to deny the religious rights of inmates. In this litigation age inmates would immediately sue the state as to the constitutionality of such a move and they would win.

That political episode, coinciding as it did with the mailing of the questionnaire, might understandably have put chaplains on the defensive, and the appearance of a survey in their mailboxes could certainly have been interpreted by some chaplains as a politically motivated attempt to measure the effectiveness of ministerial services. As a chaplain at the Summit Shock prison, I received a letter from James J. Plescia, Department of Corrections Director of Family and Ministerial Services, addressed to senior chaplains. Reflecting such a concern, he wrote:

Questions have been raised concerning the authenticity of a questionnaire about the chaplaincy experience that has been mailed recently to each of our chaplains. This will verify that Chaplain Richard Shaw is, as he states, on the staff as Chaplain at the Summit Shock Incarceration Facility, and that he has had many years experience in county jail ministry. Chaplain Shaw's interest in the health and well-being of chaplains is a wholesome interest. Research like this about chaplaincy is in short supply and, yet, it has the potential of being very useful. Those who wish to comply with Chaplain Shaw's request should feel comfortable about doing so. Please share this memorandum with your colleagues.

The letter, with its oddly phrased reference to the research project as being a "wholesome interest," along with its vague, half encouragement ("Those who wish to comply with Chaplain Shaw's request should feel comfortable about doing so") almost seemed designed to create a feeling of ambivalence. One chaplain subsequently pointed out to me that, because of the timing of the questionnaire's mailing, State administrators might have thought that it was a ploy of the churches to bring the issue before the public, and chaplains might have thought that it was a ploy by administrators to lure them into exposing their own weaknesses.

FURTHER ADVENTURES IN RESEARCH

As a follow through to the mailings, I called each facility, hoping that personal contact with at least one chaplain would spur response from the entire chaplaincy staff. This resulted in a mixed bag of conversations, a few of which helped this researcher to understand how some chaplains help to fuel the controversy about the need of their presence on the scene merely by their presence on the scene (and sometimes by their lack of presence on the scene). Many chaplains whom I contacted were extremely helpful and promised to promote the questionnaire with the other chaplains at their facility.

Others were less than helpful. A fellow Roman Catholic priest cut me off as I attempted to explain the purpose of my study, saying: "Look, I got to get going, pal." Another priest told me he was "not interested" in doing the questionnaire. At several facilities large enough for the chaplains to be full-time employees, switchboard operators informed me that the chaplains were rarely on the job. One chaplain told me not to bother pursuing a response from a fellow chaplain, saying, "He's an old man who comes in once a week and

▶ **Table 1-1: New York State Respondents Arrayed**

by Type of Facility

Government level	Number of respondents	Percent of sample
Federal Prisons	6	8.7
State Prisons	47	67.1
County and City Jails	17	24.3
Level of security		
Maximum	31	44.3
Medium	33	47.1
Minimum	6	8.6
Size of inmate population		
500 and below	15	21.4
501-999	24	34.3
1000-1499	13	18.6
1500 and above	18	25.7
Location		
Large city	15	21.4
Medium-sized city	24	20.0
Town or rural area	13	58.6
Facility for men, women, or both		
Male	55	78.6
Female	4	5.7
Both	11	15.7

sits around drinking tea." In contrast, other chaplains were unavailable by phone because they were working on the tiers with the inmates. In these instances, I explained my purpose to secretaries who assured me that they would relay my message to chaplains whom they described as being extremely involved in their ministry.

Riker's Island is not one jail, but a gigantic complex of separate facilities. I took advantage of this centralized complexity to visit the Island two weeks after mailing out the questionnaire. Ms. Irene Richards, Director of Ministerial Services, generously gave me the

▶ Table 1-2: Personal Characteristics of New York State Chaplains (Total = 70) Who Returned Initial Questionnaires

Age	Number of respondents	Percent of sample
30-39	8	11.4
40-49	19	27.0
50-59	26	37.1
60-69	14	20.3
70-79	3	4.2
Sex		
Male	60	85.7
Female	10	14.3
Race		
White	64	91.4
Black	6	8.6
Religious affiliation		
Protestant	18	25.7
Catholic	42	60.0
Jewish	7	10.0
Islamic	3	4.3
Marital Status		
Single	42	60.9
Married	34.3	24.0
Widowed or divorced	4	5.7
Years in prison/jail ministry		
1-5	28	40.0
6-10	16	22.9
11-15	16	22.9
16-20	4	5.5
21+	6	8.7

► **Table 1-3: Personal Characteristics of Federal Chaplains (Total = 113) Who Returned Second Survey's Questionnaire**

Age	Number of respondents	Percent of sample
20-29	1	0.9
30-39	33	30.0
40-49	34	30.2
50-59	28	24.8
60-69	11	9.8
70-79	0	-.-
Not indicated	6	5.3
Sex		
Male	100	88.5
Female	12	10.6
Not indicated	1	0.9
Race		
White	70	61.9
Black	19	16.8
Hispanic/Mexican	7	6.2
Other	6	5.4
Not indicated	11	9.7
Religious affiliation		
Protestant	63	55.7
Catholic	42	37.2
Jewish	1	0.9
Islamic	4	3.5
Not indicated	3	2.7
Marital status		
Single	39	34.5
Married	57	50.4
Widowed or divorced	2	1.8
Not indicated	15	13.3
Years in prison/jail ministry		
1-5	53	47.0
6-10	18	16.0
11-15	23	20.6
16-20	11	9.9
21+	6	5.4
Not indicated	2	1.1

better part of a day, touring me about the facilities on the Island and introducing me to chaplains. Very few of them had received the questionnaire. Mail is filtered through a downtown Manhattan office before it seeps its way to individual offices at the Island complex.

Ms. Richards assured me that she would attempt to track down the questionnaires, and would see that the chaplains got them even if they were lost and she had to make copies of them. The same problem regarding central office communication was borne home to me on my own turf. In my capacity as chaplain at the County Jail at the capital of New York State, I never received notice from anyone in a "front office" that the New York State Sheriff's Association was encouraging me to respond to a questionnaire which had just been sent out. In sum, on a county level, I was at the mercy of whichever clerk was in charge of distributing mail to employees within each facility.

Of the 218 questionnaires sent out 70 were completed and returned, the return rate being 32.1%. This fairly low proportion raised the question: Are these respondents representative of chaplains in general?

After examining the completed questionnaires by type of facility and by personal characteristics of the respondents, the only means of comparing data was to look at data provided by the State Department of Corrections. This allowed for comparison only with regard to sex, age, years spent in chaplaincy, and percentage of weekly work schedule. (Just as I had been assured by the Department of Corrections that it did not know the denomination of its chaplains, it assured me that it did not know the race of each chaplain. Yet, when I was hired as a state prison chaplain I had been asked to fill out a form which specifically inquired about my race.) The low number of women respondents coincided with the fact that the State's prison system employs only six female chaplains.

An Overview of Respondent Characteristics

The mean age of respondents was 52.02 years, compared with 52.1 years for all state chaplains. The only significant disproportion in the sample concerned the number of years spent in chaplaincy. The mean number of years for respondents was 9.4, while that of state chaplains in general was 4.04. Thus, those who answered the questionnaire were mainly chaplains who were more seasoned in ministry than the average chaplain in the field.

The question of representativeness is all the more pointed because, as will be seen in their composite self-portrait, the chaplains who responded to the survey gave little indications of being overly stressed by demands which their ministry placed upon them; they appeared to be mission-oriented in motivation rather than concerned about themselves, and were generally enthusiastic about their ministry. They also proved articulate and generous in offering opinions and advice in the open-ended sections of the questionnaire.

The fact that some chaplains working in facilities are less than enthusiastic and generous was borne out by the secretarial references to seldom show ministers as I called facilities in the follow up to the mailing (This writer has, in fact, worked in facilities with paid, no show chaplains.) One can only speculate as to what such chaplains would have written on a questionnaire asking them to describe their ministry, and how their returned questionnaires would have affected a portrait of chaplaincy drawn as a result of the survey.

Several chaplains, much like the one who told me not to bother to contact his fellow chaplain whom he characterized as an old man who did nothing but drink tea, gave indications that their own enthusiasm was not totally representative of other chaplains and that there were chaplains on the scene who were less than mission-oriented. One chaplain worried about his peers who "fall in love with the money or security" (40) obtained through a state salaried chaplaincy [Note 1]. Another bemoaned the existence of clergy working in prisons who are "totally unworthy to be chaplains," who are "only in for the money and . . . really don't have any concerns for the inmates" (47). One respondent discounted the idea of any composite portrait as being representative when he responded to the invitation to define the chaplaincy by saying that he "wouldn't dare because we're all so different as chaplains."

A Fierce Resistance to Participation

That there are chaplains in the system who are not articulate and not particularly politic is indicated by one return which was incomplete, uncoded as to background, and covered with a general commentary:

- A prison my friend is not jail. The way you wrote your questions will lead you to wrong conclusions. Your study will lead to nowhere unless you rewrite your questions. I do not think that you are willing to do that therefore good luck to you.
- In what prison did you see mentally ill inmates?
- [In response to the item dealing with inability to draw back emotionally] A person as such should not be a chaplain (I hope it is not you) or why do you write a question like that?
- Racial tension is to be find in any part of our society [sic]. Why should the prison be different?
- A chaplain who gets down to the C.O. [Corrections Officer] level should not be a chaplain.
- If there is friction it may be normal since communication is a major problem between people.
- Being in a prison for 8 hours is great factor in creating distress [*sic*]. Every job has its own problems.
- I did not answer your questions because it is in my opinion that your are doing the right thing in the wrong way and I am entitled to my opinion [sic].

One would hope that this chaplain is not representative of any significant number of chaplains. Nevertheless he (or she) is out there, working in a facility in an official capacity. So too is the recipient who sent back the stamped, addressed envelope filled with a handful of junk mail coupons. One cannot presume to level a negative judgement with regards to all those who failed to respond, however.

Long after the questionnaires were sent out and the returns had stopped trickling in, I attended a statewide meeting of prison chaplains. At my request, the host speaker, at a general gathering, asked the chaplains how many had answered my survey. The response was a moderate show of hands. My temptation would be to grouse about this low level of response, blaming it on the ill will of chaplains. And yet, at the risk of sounding like a Will Rogers, I never met a chaplain at the conference that I didn't like. The worst generalization I could make of those who did not respond is that they are probably people who do not like to respond to surveys.

As noted, many of those who returned the survey were, in large part, seasoned by years in chaplaincy work (37.1% having served longer than ten years). One must consider the possibility of diverging views of those who happen into, or are assigned to chaplaincy, who remain in it a short time and quit (or ask for reassignment). Would responses from these men and women have claimed a higher level of stress than that of chaplains who remain on the job for a number of years? The possibility would have to be explored in a different manner perhaps with a questionnaire sent to those who had served in chaplaincy and then left it after a short and frustrating experience. The positive tone, and the strong sense of mission which permeates the chaplains' composite self-portrait is reflective of an ideal one would want to set forth about chaplaincy. I would argue that, even if the chaplains who did respond to the survey reflect the opinions of the most dedicated chaplains, these opinions remain of great value. Just as one would listen to the most interested and dedicated lawyers for their views as to how to deal with criminal courts, so too, the chaplains who drew the self-portrait are sophisticated informants, in that they are seasoned veterans who have learned to cope with situations which many people would label as stress-producing.

Captive Subjects from the Federal System

In the Spring of 1990, after reading the completed dissertation produced by this study, Charles R. Riggs, the Chaplain Director of the Federal Bureau of Prisons, invited this writer to present workshops on job related stress for Federal Chaplains gathered at a National Convention in Phoenix, Arizona. Coinciding with this, Professor Todd Clear and Dr. Bruce D. Stout of the Graduate School of Criminal Justice at Rutgers University asked if they might use my Likert Scale in a study of their own.

This fortuitous juncture of purposes provided the opportunity to replicate the responses to the Likert Scale from my original study, this time at a "command performance" gathering of chaplains from all over the United States. One hundred and thirteen chaplains responded to the questionnaire, which was included in the packet folder handed out to each participant at the Arizona convention. Although the statistics from the Federal questionnaire could not simply be joined to those of the first without skewed results, the replication of the Likert Scale results, raising the total responses to 183 chaplains from the two studies, very much substantiated the findings of the first inquiry.

The paralleled responses (which will be presented throughout the text and in Appendix tables) followed the same patterns, and in instances where they vary, such variance can well be explained by factors which differentiate chaplaincy situations in Federal prisons from chaplaincy situations on a State and local level. The mean age of the New York State survey respondents was 52.09 years; of the Federal, 45.4 years. The years spent in chaplaincy was a 9.4 year mean for the first; 8.5 years for the Federal. In both surveys the response was predominantly Christian although the ratio changed; 60.0%/25.7% Catholic/Protestant in the New York State survey, 37.2/55.5% Catholic/Protestant for the Federal. The ratio of white to non-white respondents changed as well: 91.4% white/8.6% non-white in the first; 61.9% white/38.1% non-white in the Federal. Both sets of respondents reflect that chaplaincy is an overwhelmingly male occupation: 85.7% the New York State survey; 88.5% for the Federal.

In the responses to the Likert Scale one could see patterns which reflect factors differentiating Federal Prisons from those which are state and locally based. An obvious truism is that the Federal system is farther removed from neighborhood issues. Inmates who are in a county or metropolitan facility have concerns which are very close to the streets, and so do their chaplains.

A chaplain on a local level is more likely to be serving a neighborhood congregation and an incarcerated community who share, at least, some concerns which are geographically juxtsaposed. At the other end of the spectrum, Federal inmates, and Federal chaplains, may find themselves relocated, far from their homes, throughout the entire United States.

In this respect it makes sense that the respondents from the Federal system expressed fewer frustrations in dealing with recidivism or with mentally ill clients who drift back and forth between the streets and jail. Likewise, (as was reflected in the compared responses) it follows that Federal chaplains would experience fewer difficulties in balancing ministry to congregations outside and inside the facility, and in responding to a local ecclesiastical chain of command as well as the chain of command in their governmental employment.

In this last respect, the Federal system runs a tightly controlled organization. Reacting to this, the Federal chaplains ranked the frequency of dealing with required office duties and paper work very high (4.1 on the 5-point scale as compared to 3.3 in the New York State survey), and ranked it higher in their personal reaction to it (3.3 compared to 3.0). The Federal survey likewise recorded a higher intensity of reaction to conflicts with staff and officers (3.0 compared to 2.8) and in dealing with volunteer groups who invade their turf (3.0 compared to 2.5). These considerations impacted in the ranking of the respondents' ratings of scale items.

Similarities and Differences between State and Federal Chaplains

In the New York State survey, injustices within the system and prison overcrowding ranked first and second both in frequency of occurrence and intensity of demand. Bureaucratic paperwork demanded by the facility ranked fourth in frequency and fifth in intensity felt. In the second survey, the Federal chaplains ranked this item at the top both in frequency and demand, followed by the issues of injustice and overcrowding.

What becomes interesting or even exciting for this researcher is the repeated high ranking of the latter two issues. This was not expected when the questionnaire was devised. Issues which were expected to rank high (e.g., physical danger; the fear of contracting illnesses such as AIDS) were bypassed. In both studies the chaplains showed themselves to be influenced by what might be labeled "mission concerns." The respondents were concerned with what they wanted to accomplish, not with what might happen to them. Agreeing with the positive self-portrait culled from the responses to the New York State questionnaire, more than half of the Federal respondents in the second survey (58.4%) agreed that chaplaincy was the most important work they could ever do, even while 93.8% agreed that this ministry involves personal sacrifice for them. But an overwhelming 92.9% felt that it was important that their personality fit them for the work that they were doing, and 90.1% of them felt that they were "called" to work with prisoners.

Perhaps it is again valid to raise the objection that these chaplains speak only for the "winners" and that the losers should be heard from equally. The response of this writer is that medical and law schools fill library shelves with portraits of their winners. This study, after first presenting how others have judged chaplains and chap-

laincy in the past, purports, then, to let chaplains who are representatives of the most dedicated men and women in the field, have
their own day in court.

NOTE

1. The returned questionnaires were number-coded, not so that the chaplains
might be identified, but rather so that the individual statements of chaplains
might be read in the context of background data. The numerical code and
corresponding data about the respondents are recorded at the end of the text as
Appendix III.

Chapter 2

HISTORICAL PERSPECTIVES ON THE PRISON CHAPLAINCY

In prison literature, much is made of the fact that "Penitentiaries," as the name implies, were designed by religious idealists. Pope Clement XI, in the 18th century, is credited with creating the first juvenile reformatory, where punishment and education were combined into one program. In England, Jeremy Bentham's ideas for the reformation of criminals were concretized in prisons where periods of solitude were balanced with periods of daily religious instruction. As noted by Mark Benney in *Gaol Delivery*, the system "staked everything on the task of turning convicted criminals into saintly church goers. If it failed in this, it failed in everything" (1948:109).

THE MORE REMOTE PAST

In the United States the Quakers are credited with giving birth to the penitentiary which flourished as a concept if not a fact during the nineteenth century. Americans thought of themselves as a religious people — specifically a Christian, Protestant people — and the power of Protestant denominations in shaping societal norms and political policies was considerable. On a level where decisions were made about the running of public institutions — the level at which trustees and boards of directors met — prominent clergymen possessed a great amount of power. One of the most visible of these was the Rev. Louis Dwight (d. 1854), who drew both applause and enmity from his sometime role as minister to inmates and sometime role as a political figure fighting vituperatively against those whose views about prison policies clashed with his own (McKelvey, 1977:54).

And yet, despite their power on a policy-making level, the influence of clergymen within facilities was often more circumscribed than might be expected. Chaplains who served in institutions were not necessarily welcome members of a staff, and the presence of religious influences and practices were oftentimes considered to be a hindrance to the smooth and orderly administration of a facility.

Interesting because its publishing date is so early, a book about Vermont's Windsor Prison, written in 1834, notes of the institution, that "twenty years after its foundation, nothing like a Sabbath school Bible class had ever been introduced — and that at no time had there been more than one short sermon in a week, and sometimes only one or two in the course of a year." Although a chapel had been included in the original building, "scarcely had the dust fallen on its seats before it was converted into a place of daily labor, and the altar of religious worship set up in a cellar." When, at one point, the inmates petitioned for religious services they were told that the administration "had tried everywhere within proper distance of the prison but could not get a single preacher to visit that place and do the duty of a chaplain" (Reynolds, 1834:10:106).

Even the Quakers encountered a hostile reception in the very institution which was their brainchild. Harry Barnes, in *The Evolution of Penology in Pennsylvania*, observes:

> The first recorded activity of the society was the introduction, in 1787, of religious services into the Walnut Street Jail. The keeper of the jail did all in his power to prevent the innovation, and gave a sullen consent only on the written command of the sheriff of the county. The prisoners were assembled in the jail yard. A cannon was placed beside the improvised pulpit and a gunner stood by with a lighted match ready to fire into the mass of convicts at any sight of a riot (Barnes, 1968:85).

The Rev. John Clay, a British prison chaplain whose memoirs provide a compassionate and balanced view of Nineteenth Century Chaplaincy, noted of the situation in his own country wherein state and church were so intrically enmeshed: "Chapels and chaplains were seldom part of the prison establishment. Some loose parson, of insolvent tendencies, was commonly hired, at a cheap rate, for the office of ordinary" (1861:17). In *Prison Secrets: Things Seen, Suffered and Recorded during Seven Years in Ludlow Street Jail*, a one-time inmate recalls his first Sunday of incarceration when the chaplain's arrival was announced by a guard with the yell: "Put the place in order, damn it, the clergyman is at the door!" The minister, accompanied by volunteers from his church, conducted a service to the prisoners who had been congregated into a hallway to hear him. When the service was finished, "hardly had the massive door that separates the prison from the good mission closed, than many of the recently pious faces underwent a change, and as if to make up for lost time, their owners filled the air with hideous roars and general imprecations" (MacDonald, 1893:35-37).

"This Obscure Office"

There were vocal critics who questioned the value of attempting to salvage criminals. Alexis de Toqueville, while praising the intentions of those "taking upon themselves this obscure office," and noting that they might earn the veneration of all who knew them, nonetheless felt that "yet they sometimes deceive themselves respecting the results of their efforts." He saw the regeneration, "the radical change of a wicked person into an honest man" as so difficult that "if it ever takes place, [it] must be very rare" (DeBaumont and de Tocqueville, 1964:86-87). In other words, the prison chaplain was to be classified as an irrelevant, dewy-eyed dreamer.

A chaplain writing in 1860 concurred with de Toqueville's view of, at least, the prisoners when he observed: "I find that the men generally are more anxious concerning their release from confinement than their delivery from the bondage of sin" (Ayers, 1964:61). Chaplains had to deal with hardened cynicism on the part of inmates, and when such sinful practices as card playing were forbidden, resourceful inmates would adapt to the situation and replace the confiscated cards by making new ones out of pages ripped from distributed Bibles (Benney, 1948:105). Rev. John Clay, in spite of years of dedicated service to prisoners, agreed that preaching to many of them was "mere casting of pearls before swine; the drunkenness and promiscuous intercourse among the prisoners would have thwarted the most zealous chaplain" (1861:17).

The fear of violence which led the Walnut Street Jail administrators to conduct services at cannon point was real enough, and congregating prisoners was a natural invitation to trouble. A British ex inmate, writing at the turn of the century, recorded a case in point:

Every now and then extraordinary scenes used to occur in chapel and we sometimes had a fight to vary the ceremony. One Sunday, soon after the death of Queen Victoria, the priest was speaking about her and referred to her as having been the ruler of one of the greatest empires the world has ever known, an Empire in which there was more freedom and justice than in any other country. All at once a man jumped up and began raving and storming, declaring there was no law or justice in England. For a minute it looked as if he would knock the priest down, but he was speedily removed by the officers (W.B.N., 1903:98).

At the Eastern Penitentiary of Pennsylvania at Cherry Hill, "religious services, which were advocated by the founders to an almost fanatical degree, were seriously hampered since the ministers were obliged to call on each prisoner one at a time to impart the Gospel. The unfavorable circumstances under which these sermons were delivered, allowed the convicts to sleep or read during the preaching and, preventing them from seeing the preacher or hearing him distinctly, have served to destroy most of whatever value may be held to reside in these religious exercises" (Barnes, 1968:351). Only after 1831 was an arrangement made whereby a minister could stand at the end of a tier and preach to inmates in a row of cells all at one time. Moreover, the legislature was tardy in appropriating funds for religious and educational purposes. The law of 1829 provided for an unsalaried chaplain but the Board of Inspectors found it impossible to fill the post. When a chaplain was finally found there was an ironic besiegement of the legislature by citizens "urging that the office be discontinued for fear of proselytizing" (Teeters and Shearer, 1957:151).

Badly Printed Bibles, and Not a Dime More

An observer in *ante bellum* Alabama complained that, except for a limited supply of "badly printed Bibles . . . not a dime has ever been expended by authority of the legislature in furnishing the miserable inmates of the penitentiary with knowledge or the means of reformation of any kind, either religiously or morally" (Ayers, 1984:60). The same author notes that after the wars and the freeing of the black population it became almost impossible to find white chaplains to serve black inmates.

Since legislatures refused to assign black preachers as chaplains the black inmates were left to the necessity of preaching the Gospel to themselves — an interesting prelude to the prison birth, in the next century, of the "Nation of Islam" movement. At first, religious services provided by the state were virtually restricted not only to whites but to Protestant whites. In this respect, the penal system of the United States reflected that of its mother country, England, with its established Anglican religion. If Protestantism was not established as an official religion in law it was, nevertheless, established as such by the consensus of the strongly Nativist American population. Oscar Handlin, writing of Massachussetts during the era of the great wave of Irish immigration, noted:

> Despite laws to restrict their influence, Protestant chaplains dominated the spiritual life of public institutions, controlling the inmates' reading material and religious services, while Catholic priests found great difficulty in securing access even after a resolve of the legislature in 1858 admitted them (1977:161).

In Albany, New York, the city's first Catholic Bishop, Francis McCloskey, used his considerable diplomatic skills to gain the entry of Catholic priests, previously barred, into the Albany Penitentiary. New York City's Archbishop John Cardinal Hughes formed a lifelong friendship with Governor William Seward when the latter flew in the face of Nativist sentiment to overrule and reverse the decision of Sing Sing's warden, who had denied a priest a visit to see an inmate sentenced to hang. Journals of nineteenth century chaplains afford evidence that the attitude of ministers was to save the immigrants from the errors of their own religion rather than allow them access to it. One such chaplain kept a journal listing such observations as:

> No. 877. Thomas Foley, Ireland. An Irish Catholic. From the Scriptures has obtained a knowledge of true religion and rejects the superstition of Popery. Knows that without regeneration he cannot enter the kingdom of Heaven.

> No. 882. Patrick McGuken, Ireland; seems hopelessly under influence of superstition. Is visited by the priest (Teeters and Shearer, 1957:154).

Finlay of Ohio

The Rev. James B. Finlay, chaplain at the Ohio Penitentiary, himself salaried, told Catholic inmates that priests did not come to see them regularly because they did not get money for doing so. Finlay's memoirs stand as an example of a type of autobiographical literature which makes searching for history a matter of wandering through a smokescreen. His recollections are a continual paean of self-praise. He records a succession of unbroken successes in the work of reclaiming souls, with no failures recorded but for those inmates who were so firmly in the grip of the devil (or the Catholic Church) as to be classified as culpably obtuse. He further butters his bread by carefully praising the virtues of his employers. He assures his readers that "never perhaps in any part of the world was there a set of officers having the management of a prison who possessed and manifested more of the spirit of Christian philanthropy toward their degenerate but important charges than the officers of the institution" (1974:6).

Perhaps such obsequiousness was indeed necessary for effectiveness, for while clergy who were powerful enough to serve as trustees held clout, the parsons employed in individual institutions were under the thumbs of their employers. As noted in a contemporary description of Sing Sing: "The inspectors appoint the warden, the chaplain and the doctor, and also have the power to dismiss them" (Erikson, 1976:57). Few, if any, chaplains were in a comfortable position to play an adversarial role in the facility in which they worked.

Rev. John Clay seems to have been tempered by the crucible of chaplaincy into a saintly and heroic man. Clear-eyed about the lack of natural piety in his charges, he could, nonetheless, write at the end of his life (1861:340, 614, 390): "We are in fact, at last learning that God is the ruler of this world as of the next ... We are at last beginning to believe that the Saviour came to save, not only men's souls, but, literally, the world." Of the frustrations of trying to preach of God's love within a framework of punishment, he wrote:

> While the prisoner is in a state of irritation and anger from the smart of the sharp deterrents, it is inconsistently expected that the chaplain should reform him! But the chaplain is not in the right place amidst whips, cranks, tread wheels and other restraints of bodily pain, and he feels the message of mercy with which he is charged cannot be effectively delivered to the prisoner when everything about him savours of spite and vindictiveness.

In other sections of his memoirs he captures perfectly the frustrations of prison chaplaincy:

> Can many such clergymen be expected to offer themselves when it is manifest that in entering on a gaol chaplaincy they choose a path of duty which, however well they may pursue it, never leads to professional advancement...And with regard to Episcopal favor, some time will elapse before the nature, and I am bold to say the value of labors such as ours, will be taken into consideration. Unfortunately, our obscure but incessant work among ignorant and vicious outcasts, leaves us little time to edit a Greek play, or write a pamphlet on a theological controversy.

Clay's Critique on the Exaggeration of Successes

Clay's book stands in stark contrast to the defensive memoirs of such men as the Rev. James B. Finlay who would have readers believe that his chaplaincy was a succession of constant triumphs. Of such claims Clay wrote: "Chaplains have, beyond doubt, exaggerated their success. They have, in fact, been themselves deceived. And of this, unquestionably one cause has been the acceptance of mere physical emotions and manifestations as true repentance." He adds, with an eye towards chaplaincy and politics: "It is feared, however, that the chaplain is sometimes, rather, the deceiver than the deceived" (1861:390.391).

The claims of absolute success by men such as Rev. Finlay were more than just an attempt to make themselves look good and to please their employers. The stakes were much greater than that. A great deal of stock had been put into the prison system's ability to reform criminals, and this by religionists who preached that the means to do so were through the power of the Gospel. To deny that this was possible was to strike at the very heart of the Christian message. Much energy and expense had been invested in the American concept of the penitentiary system. It was not easy to admit a general defeat.

It was little wonder that men like Finlay painted a rosy picture to convince the public, and perhaps even themselves, that their efforts were not in vain. After the initial era of reform in the penal system, overcrowding and the punitive practices of authoritarian regimes caused the old belief in the conversion of criminals to fade. The simple warehousing of prisoners became the order of the day. Some institutions such as Brockway did away with the office of chaplain, and the general cynical attitude, voiced by Hastings H. Hart of Minnesota, was that "no convict ought to be allowed to feel for a moment that he can make a gain of godliness" (McKelvey, 1977:146).

In general, during the latter part of the nineteenth century, the quality of chaplaincy depended upon the quality of the men working in this hidden ministry. Some showed little interest in their work, as was noted by one inspector's report: "The moral tone of the convicts here is as high as could be expected under the circumstances, though we regret our inability to refer your excellency to any report of the chaplain, that office having failed up to this time to render any" (Ayers, 1984:207).

A Preference for Itinerants

In 1910, in a work called *Prison Reform*, Charles R. Henderson wrote off the importance of religion in prisons, saying: "I have found the resident chaplain to be less desireable for religious ministrations than an itinerant service. One mind, and that the mind of the reformatory governor, must have and hold and wield every operating agency — impel, steady and direct the whole, and every item of the procedure" (1910:67).

The denigration of the chaplains' role is reflected in the comment of one clergyman of that era who noted a minister preaching behind bars met "duty enough to tax all the brain and talents God has given him; and yet he is met by men, professed Christians, and even ministers, with this inquiry: 'What good are you doing with all your labors?'"(Ayers, 1984:207).

The notion of the uselessness of the chaplains' role was reinforced in a history of San Quentin, in a description of a minister who served that institution during the 1880s. According to the history, a white haired, 70-year-old parson named Cummings "wandered around San Quentin in well meaning bewilderment, blundering into the corral around the cell blocks when he had no business to be there, buying tickets home for discharged convicts, going to Sacramento to plead for pardons for other men still imprisoned, and even recommending to the warden an informal discharge for a prisoner who claimed to be unjustly convicted."

The warden, Judge Ames, "embarked on a campaign to harass the chaplain until his life would become so miserable he would leave of his own accord. A number of humiliating incidents, some large and some small, were added to the chaplain's store of bitterness." Ames had the man moved from the chaplain's house into a run down shack. On one occasion when Cummings addressed Ames with the words, "Judge, I think," the warden said, harshly and in the presence of convicts and freemen, "You have no right to think, Sir" (Lamott, 1961:135).

A Transatlantic Perspective

Writing about England during the nineteenth century, an observer of that nation's criminal justice system noted: "The established Church has a tacit agreement not to question the state's views about wrongdoing, which enables the latter to lean heavily and confidently on the Divine principle when justifying its use of sanctions" (Benney: 1948:7). In the United States at the same time, Protestant chaplains, employees of the system, were in much the same uncomfortable position of being forced to give "tacit agreement" to administration policies. As the American nation grew into a gradual acceptance of its pluralistic population and chaplains of other denominations and faiths joined the ranks of the Protestant ministers, the ministers were not freed from their uncomfortable state controlled position. Rather, the clergy of other religious groups joined them in an equal sharing of that uncomfortable position.

It was the increase in numbers of immigrant Catholics within the nation's prisons which in time gained Catholic priests access to these institutions and at length official status as government employees. In the interim, before they were employed, Catholic clergymen could at least enjoy freedom from being controlled by the system and could even bask in the advantage of sharing with the inmates a sense of being despised and held in suspicion by the authorities. As would be the case with Islamic Imams in the next century, this placed priests in the advantageous situation of being easily heroized by those they served. They were free — as free as Paul the Apostle preaching in the prisons of the Roman Empire.

Mainstream Protestantism vs. Fundamentalist Religion

By the 1890s this began to change. "Chapel services were generally under the direction of full time Protestant chaplains, but Catholic priests were permitted to minister to inmates of their Faith. By the end of the period some of the states with increasing Catholic populations were officially naming Catholics as assistant chaplains" (McKelvey, 1977:185).

"Assistant" may have been an entrance through a back door, but the entry soon allowed Catholic clergymen to be as owned and controlled by the system as their predecessors. Others who found entry through the back door at the end of the nineteenth century were predecessors of the "full Gospel" fundamentalist, born agains. Too loosely organized and independent to be as controlled by authorities as the mainline churches, they found a ready-made inmate audience by appealing with a highly emotional, "born again" conversion experience. An early forerunner of this sort of religious grouping was the organization run by Mrs. Maud Ballington Booth, who broke with the Salvation Army to form the Volunteer Prison League, which gave converted inmates a badge to wear (presumably different than that worn by guards) and pledged them to read the Bible, use clean language, "form cheerful habits," and obey the prison rules (McKelvey: 1977:186).

THE PROGRESSIVE ERA

During the nineteenth century, all educational efforts (and these were few) and libraries were provided under the direction of chaplains. Thus, "practically all of the books in these libraries were religious in nature, and in all probability were intended to compel prisoners to contemplate the eternal sufferings to which they would be subjected if they did not repent" (Roberts, 1971:162). The rise of the Progressive movement, however, brought a new set of players into the prison field — social workers, psychologists, and educators whose efforts were not intended to reform in a theological sense, but to rehabilitate within a social reality. Because these new workers moved into a field occupied by chaplains they necessarily collided with these clergymen whose patterns of work were threatened by their presence. Assessing the reduction in role, Michael Wolff in his book *Prison* wrote:

> Just as in the outside world the development of the welfare state has greatly diminished the Church's responsibilities and opportunities for tending the physical needs of the people, so the chaplain's task has come to be limited to providing for the spiritual welfare of those in his charge; and even here the line between the medico-psychiatric treatment and religious or spiritual healing is often difficult to detect (1967:254).

Writing in 1936, Sanford Bates observed:

> With the separation of duties it appeared to us that the ministry of chaplain in a penal institution had entirely changed. The prison school had been taken over by the trained educationalists. Family contacts were handled by the social workers and the libraries staffed by trained librarians. Apparently there was nothing else but religion for the chaplain to busy himself about, and that could be done on Sunday in an hour or two (1936:163).

The diminution of moral reformation as a goal within the criminal justice system and the resultant diminishment of the role of the chaplain in the public's estimation is well captured by Giles Playfair in *The Punitive Obsession*:

> It seems likely that in the public's mind, and certain that in the judiciary's mind, psychiatry has replaced religious instruction as the treatment means relied on for the rehabilitation of a considerable number of prisoners. He would be a very eccentric judge today who justified a prison sentence on the ground that he was giving the offender (man or boy) a chance to repent of his sins under the expert and devoted guidance of a chaplain. On the other hand, a person who commits some non-acquisitive and therefore apparently motiveless sort of crime which is not so outrageous that the judge compulsively and conveniently falls back on "wickedness" as its only explanation, is likely to be assured that "the best possible psychiatric care" awaits him in prison (1971:220).

Rehabilitation to the Foreground

At first, the takeover of rehabiltation, both in concept and in actual work, by social workers, educators, and psychologists, shunted the chaplains aside. Then, many clergy involved in prison ministry rallied, responded to the new age, and joined rather than fought the newcomers. Some of the newcomers, in turn, found the chaplains to be welcome members of a team. "Within the framework of religious terminology," wrote Elmer Johnson in *Crime, Correction and Society*, "some inmates will accept the role of treatment client and will not resist the principles of therapy, whereas they would be repelled by the specialized language of professional therapy. For this reason, one trend in correction has been to place more emphasis on a trained chaplaincy, well grounded in sociology and psychology, as well as theology" (1968:589).

Sheldon Glueck (1959), in *The Problem of Delinquency*, notes this development in chaplaincy, pointing out that "in the past it was customary to assign retired or misfit clergy to institutional chaplaincies." He includes an article by a chaplain at a correctional institution who is a member of a diagnostic team made up of a social worker, psychiatrist, and psychologist. The chaplain, the Rev. J. L. Cedarleaf, points out the difference between a neurotic faith and a creative faith, the latter providing a means of holistic growth.

Within the therapeutic process, Cedarleaf claims that it is the "distinct kind of transference that occurs in relation to the chaplain that makes him a unique person on the team." Within the realm of that which is specifically religious, Cedarleaf distinguishes between ultimate and finite goals, saying:

> It is because the chaplain deals with boys whose problems are largely finite that he must utilize treatment processes which are designed by psychology and social work, in order that a solid foundation may be laid, from which the boy can build with the help of others, a secure and abiding faith in God, that will give him courage to face the most serious and disturbing concerns of his existence (1959:770).

The inclusion of the chaplain as a member of a professional team was (wherever it existed) a mixed blessing. According to David Fogel in *We Are the Living Proof*, it tended to separate the chaplain from the lives of those within the institutions, both staff and inmates. Cynically, he observed that "the guards also noticed that the reformative personnel worked 9 A.M. to 5 P.M., Monday through Friday, and were secure in their offices and chapels" (1975:74). Although Fogel felt that "chaplains and other religious enthusiasts were equally certain that they held the key to unlock the door to the reformation" of prisons, they were nonetheless not that secure in their offices and chapels as he thought. In *Chronicles of San Quentin*, Kenneth Lamott noted, in passing, that "In 1922 the Protestant Chaplain was fired for kiting out a manuscript containing the life story of the notorious murderer, Bluebeard Watson" (1961:196). In agreement with Fogel, Philip Priestley observed that guards, who traditionally liked to represent a moral order which kept inmate-staff relationships in the easily understood bad guy vs. good guy roles, resented the new professionalism brought in by the Progressive Era. He wrote:

> The chaplain, the medical officer, the prison visitor, the tutor organizer, all brought with them expertise based on training which was external to the prison. All, in turn, were put in their places, denied effective shares in the distribution of power and squeezed into conformist roles on the staff side of the institutional equation (1980:10).

Rabbi Julius Leibert, who served as chaplain at San Quentin, Folsom, and Alcatraz, was firmly supportive of the professional staff. However, he saw the danger of including the chaplain with them as a united group. He wrote:

> In my opinion, formalized religion is a dubious factor in therapy, especially under present conditions. Sponsored by the prison authorities, it is generally identified with them. Moralizing falls on deaf ears. The emphasis of the parole

board on mere chapel attendance has the effect, for a good many prisoners, of relegating religion to the same category as occupational therapy or work on the jute mill" (in Leibert with Kingsberg, 1965:211).

Chaplains and the Professional Staff

The joining together of the chaplains with the professional staff also tended to heighten some of the tensions which already existed in a non-ecumenical age. In California, a Governor's committee investigating San Quentin "observed with distaste the guerilla warfare that was going on between the chaplains and the psychiatrists, and between the Protestant and [the] Catholic Chaplains" (Lamott, 1961:248).

In facilities where the chaplaincy was kept separate from the professional staff (and where chaplains were thus not involved in time-consuming secular responsibilities), some observers saw an advantage in the employment of clergy who shared their prison duties with outside parish work. Writing of such part-time chaplaincy, Ann D. Smith argued:

> Extension of welfare and after care services has relieved the chaplain of many visits and reports which were formally his responsibility. It is therefore more practicable to employ a part time chaplain who can bring ideas and experiences from his parish into a community which is of necessity cut off from such contacts. He is able to provide a valuable link with the outside world which will increase rather than decrease his spiritual influence on the prisoners (1962:276).

A seemingly permanent rift began to develop between chaplains who accepted the importance of professional therapeutic and rehabilitative means, and those chaplains who, in the manner of television Evangelist Jimmy Swaggart, heap scorn on the idea of psychology and who depend instead solely on the healing power of faith. Writes Elmer Johnson:

> Through specialized training, the chaplain is prepared to understand and administer the therapeutic assets of religion. Other chaplains oppose this trend to transform them into "junior- grade social workers." They agree that the chaplains should understand the work of other prison departments, but they see their proper roles to be providers for religious worship and dispensers of "the truths of God" (1968:589).

A PROLIFERATION OF RELIGIONS

With mainline denomination chaplains firmly fixed as members of staff and often forced to play a carefully restricted role by reason of being employees of the system, such chaplains found themselves competing more and more with volunteer evangelists of a fundamentalist type.

Fundamentalist Voluntary Evangelism

These included such groups as the Full Gospel Businessmen's Association, Chaplain Ray's Prison Fellowship, and Chuck Colson's Prison Ministries. The fundamentalist approach can sometimes be greatly appealing to an inmate seeking a dramatic "turn around" or "Born again" experience which can be far more emotionally satisfying than the routine, business-as-usual services offered by the official chaplains. As well, because these groups are comprised of outside-the-institution volunteers, there is the appeal for the inmates of relating to religious groups which can be seen as separate from and even adversarial to prison staff and administration and to the whole machinery of the criminal justice system.

The oftentimes successful fundamentalist ministries were bad enough competition for the official chaplains. Worse was the development and growth of religions born within the prisons. Mail order ministry certificates and home-grown mini-sects have always presented a perplexing issue with regards to such questions as tax exemption status, and the minimum standard rules of prison which allow for the practice of one's religion as a basic right.

Even the ancient Catholic Church can sometimes create confusion in some bureaucratic minds. After he was arrested in a right-to-life protest, New York's Bishop Austin Vaughn was required to spend some time in our jail. While he was incarcerated, I was forbidden to bring him an ounce of wine so that he could say daily mass. That decision was reversed only in the fact of strong public reaction to the denial to the elderly Bishop this 2000-year-old ritual of faith.

CONS – The Church of the New Song

In contrast, imprisoned Rastafarians gain little public sympathy when they insist that the smoking of marijuana is a ritualistic part of their religion, a use which is at least in the same religious ballpark as the ritualist use of wine by Christian and Jewish groups. One prison-born religion which challenged traditional religious prerogatives won a surprising, but logically consistent decision from the United States Supreme Court. The inmates who developed the religion, "Cons" (Church of the New Song), decided that their rituals had to include the use of Harvey's Bristol Cream sherry and filet mignon. In *Therault v. Carlson*, the court decided against prison officials who refused to accept the possibility that the Church of the New Song could be a "real" religion. The decision noted:

> The court is not unmindful of the very real possibility that petitioners are still engaging in a game and attempting to perpetuate a colossal fraud upon both this court and the Federal prison system. Nevertheless, with all due respect to the respondent, the court cannot declare petitioner's religion illegitimate (Berkmans, 1979:46-47).

The rise of Islam in the United States followed a different pattern. When it first appeared in prisons during the 1930s its expression was racist and violent. As the Ku Klux Klan used the Bible and became a racist caricature of Christianity, so in a reverse bigotry, black Muslims used the Koran in the same manner, deploying it as a means of expressing hatred against the white race. Prisons provided fertile ground for such a movement to get started. The needs of blacks in prison had long been ignored by white prison administrators. In an account, itself tinged with racism, of the history of Southern, black penal camps, Blake McKelvey notes:

> It was difficult to secure white chaplains and it was out of the question to hire Negroes. However, plenty of the latter turned up in the camps by legal proceeding, and these dusky but fluent souls usually practiced their calling without restraint on the one day of rest (1977:209).

By moving into the realm of a religion which was, for all practical purposes, virtually unknown in the United States, black inmates could develop an identity which separated them from a cultural expression of Christianity which had become part of a white controlled caste system.

The Rise of the World Community of Islam in the West

During the 1930s, under the leadership of Chicago-based Elijah Muhammed, the self-named "Nation of Islam" preached: "The white man is morally bankrupt; a doomed devil" (Butler, 1978:55). As years passed, however, an internal spiritual growth occurred within the black Muslim movement which reflected the earlier conversion of entire peoples to Christianity by means of conquest (e.g., the native peoples of Latin America). If, at first, such converts belonged to such a new religion only in name, successive generations of these peoples grew into it as a true faith experience.

Wallace Muhammed, the son of Elijah, moderated his father's teachings and changed the name of his group from the exclusivist sounding "Nation of Islam" to the more universal "World Community of Islam in the West." He declared that his religious group would differ from other Islamic groups "only as Congregationalists differ from Methodists." Wallace allowed whites to join the religion, and acknowledged that "prison officials in the past had a right to be frightened. We called all Caucasians devils. If we call them all devils, how could they feel safe with us" (Butler, 1978:56).

Such mellowing on the level of the core of the black Muslim movement did not change a reality which continued to exist among offshoots of the movement and which still exists as of this writing. Just as the Ku Klux Klan still raises a fiery cross as a sign of its peculiar expression of a racist quasi-Christianity, so too, racist blacks in prisons, oftentimes gathering under the name "Five Percenters," adhere to a violent creed of hatred of all whites in the name of Allah.

As the presence of Ku Kluxers is an embarrassment of Christians, so too the presence of the Five Percenters embarrasses and causes great problems for Islamic believers who have difficulty in getting prison officials to see a difference between the two groups. Ronald Berkmans, in *Opening the Gates: The Rise of the Prisoner's Movement*, notes that "the Muslims shared with the early Christian community a profound sense of other-directedness" (1979:52). Like the early Christians who lived under the shadow of governments wed to official state religions, so too, the Muslims existed, in past decades, and to a great extent still exist, as outsiders in a system which is wed to the mainline, American-blessed, groupings of Protestant-Catholic-Jewish religions and chaplaincies.

Interestingly, Islamics in the twentieth century exist within institutions in much the same status as did Roman Catholics in the United States during the nineteenth century era of Nativism. Just as the growing numbers of Catholic immigrants within institutions were denied access to "Papist" clergy who had to win their right to gain entry, so too, the same battle had to be fought by Islamics. At first, Islamics were denied the right to religious services, clergy visits, and Islamic literature. They eventually responded by bringing the issue to the courts, and in 1964, in *Sostre v. McGinnis*, won a landmark U.S. Supreme Court decision which acknowledged that they enjoyed the same rights as any other religious denomination. A 1970 manual on jail administration issued by the National Sheriff's Association reflects the impact of this decision when it notes: "The present state of the case law with respect to religious practice rights in the prison and jail setting has evolved largely because of the growth in recent years of the black Muslim movement" (Walrod 1970:62).

Stridency and Separatism?

This breakthrough decision was tempered, however, by the reality that officials still insist upon seeing the presence of Islamics as a cloak for violence. Written six years after *Sostre v. McGinnis,* a study of Illinois jails observed: "Of the one hundred and fifty four jails which permit clergymen to visit inmates, six expressly limit visiting privileges to "bonafide' religions; two of those expressly exclude black Muslims" (Mattick and Sweet, 1970:217).

In a 1978 article, "The Muslims are No Longer an Unknown Quantity," it is acknowledged that, even after their legal victories, imprisoned Muslims remain "strange, strident, and separatist." Their presence aggravated the long standing problem that, religion, in general, becomes a battleground within facilities. As the article notes:

Wardens have in recent years become sceptical of assemblies of worshiping inmates. There is, generally speaking, no less religious group of men than prison inmates. Few attend the prison chapels, and, if they do, prison officials feel they can safely assume that their main purpose is not to worship, but to foment disorder, or to exchange drugs, or to have homosexual trysts (Butler, 1978:57).

Wardens, despite *Sostre v. McGinnis*, can and do cite *Brown v. McGinnis* in saying that "Prisoners might have an absolute right to believe as they wish, but, where the practice of their religion interferes with legitimate prison or jail goals such as security and discipline, it may be regulated by the authorities" (Walrod, 1970:60).

Because this situation remains a strong factor in the relations between Islamic groups and wardens, the role of Islamic chaplains is of special interest. In one sense they are freed, as were Catholic clergymen before they won official acceptance, of living under the blessing and control of the administrators of institutions. They enjoy much the same freedom as the volunteer groups of fundamentalist Gospel preachers. In the eyes of the inmates, they are not only not a part of the system, but, like the inmates themselves, they are often harassed and even persecuted. In short, by sharing persecution with the inmates, they may enjoy far greater credibility than do the officially controlled chaplains of mainline denominations.

Chapter 3

STATUS AND REPUTATION OF THE CHAPLAINCY

The present-day norm, that a chaplain works under the control of the administration of a facility, is reflected in a 1982 report of a "Full Service Chaplaincy Program" published in *Innovations in South Carolina Law Enforcement*. A ten-page description of the chaplain portrays him as a sort of ombudsman and public relations man, but more for the sake of the officers and staff than for the inmates. Included in that which is "expected" of the chaplain are the following items:

- The lieutenant or sergeant in charge shall be informed of the chaplain's presence, preferably by the appearance of the chaplain at role call.
- Chaplains shall not interfere with officers but shall be ready to assist officers at the officer's request and discretion.
- No chaplain shall carry a weapon while primarily active as a chaplain. However, a chaplain may be a reservist upon proper training.

Chaplains are also expected to:

- Provide counselling to inmates upon request.
- Attend Department award ceremonies, social events, etc.
- Be on call as available to respond to emergencies.
- Assist in conducting memorial services and other religious ceremonies upon request.
- Visit officers and their families in hospitals (Metts and Cook, 1982:7-8).

The foregoing is a portrait of a person totally controlled by administration. Little wonder that Timothy Fitzharris, writing in *The Desirability of a Correctional Ombudsman*, characterizes chaplains as belonging within the system, but doesn't bother to consider them as potential ombudsman candidates. His candidate for the role would by an "independent reviewer" whose "forte is communication." He hopes that with such a person "prisoners would have a means of voicing their complaints without fear of reprisal, and immeasurable benefits should accrue for giving prisoners the feeling that someone is really listening" (Fitzharris, 1973:69). One would want to think that this description would fit a chaplain. One also hopes that Fitzharris, writing in California, took time for a second look at chaplains after a bill which would have created an ombudsman position in the state's prison system was vetoed by Governor Ronald Reagan on the grounds that such a position would be "divisive" (1973:xvii).

CONFUSED AND VARYING EXPECTATIONS

At present the role of a chaplain is one of confused and varying expectations. Moreover, as a number of authors note, the role and effectiveness of clergymen in corrections depends almost totally on "the quality of the individual chaplain" (Smith, 1962:278). As observed by Elmer Johnson:

> He may be a man with an eighth grade education, preaching a religion of guilt and fear. He may be defined as a "jack-of-all-trades," serving as a court of last resort for prisoner grievances and then joining the guards, billy club in hand, in a time of emergency. At the other extreme, he may have both a psychiatric and a theological degree, working as a well accepted member of the treatment team (1974:588).

Balancing these contrasts between the extremes described, W. Marlin Butts of Oberlin College, after spending ten years in training chaplains for prison ministry, decided that between the heights of professionalism and the depths of ineffectiveness, "I'm afraid that the greater number fall at the lower end" (1966:75). Others portray a more positive picture. Max Grunhut, in *Penal Reform*, sees the "rivalry of secular and spiritual forces" as being a hidden blessing. Kept more and more to the religious sphere, no longer sidetracked by the running of libraries and recreational programs "the Church has gained by an intensification of her effort." Whether or not rehabilitation is or is not a goal in prisons, "it is the inalienable right and obligation of the Church to bring her message to every man, whether in prison or not. This obtains even if the state pursues no reformative object" (1972:255).

Rabbi William Leffler shares this aggressive stance, extending the missionizing task to include as targets those in charge of running facilities. In an article entitled, "On Being Human in the Prison Community," he insists that officers and administrators must be trained toward this goal. Leffler asserts that "the staff will have to start thinking of prisoners as their brothers in the Biblical sense of the word — as created in the image of God" (1973:154). Distinguished criminologist Daniel Glaser points to an important fact to show "how much greater is the rehabilitative impact of prison chaplains compared to holders of other staff positions." He writes:

It is striking that of the successful releases who credited a specific staff member with being a major influence in their reformation one sixth cited the prison chaplains and religious workers, although these employers constitute only a fraction of the total prison staff (1964:145).

Glaser also notes that chaplains are "a leading source of non-criminal ties between a prisoner and the outside world. Inmates have the time, and frequently are in a mood which makes them amenable to conversion to a new conception of the spiritual meaning of their lives and of their relationship to mankind and to their God" (1964:283). J. E. Hall Williams, in *Changing Prisons*, joins in this revisionist view of chaplaincy. Anticipating a "holistic" approach to rehabilitation, he points out that the once shunted aside clergy may have a role to play after all:

Not all prisoners will be influenced by the chaplains. Clearly only a small minority attend services. But for a few the chaplain provides a ready counsellor and confidant, and the religion he professes constitutes a considerable source of support and comfort for some prisoners. It is possible that sufficient thought has not been given to the role of the chaplain in a modern prison system (1975:131).

Granted that there is a vital role for chaplains to play, the problem remains that the quality of chaplaincy is very much dependent upon the quality of individual chaplains, and, as observers have pointed out, in the past prisons and jails have served as dumping grounds for lesser lights in the clergy, just as they have served as dumping grounds for misfits in society at large.

Chaplains as Seen by Prison/Jail Administration and Staff

If the recruitment of quality chaplains remains an important issue, so too does the importance of the acceptance of the role of chaplains by those who run and staff facilities. Rev. James E. Post, Protestant chaplain of Kansas State Penitentiary, noted of the chaplains' relationship with those in charge of the institutions:

A chaplain must not undertake his work with any misconceptions about the manner in which he will be received. He may find, for example, that the warden or certain guards resent his presence. He may be looked upon as a "do-gooder" and be informed that he will not be allowed "to run the prison" and that he will be tolerated only so long as he remains within a restricted role as a spiritual advisor (1968:95).

Norman Fenton, who spent half a century working in the California Department of Corrections and served as that state's Deputy Director of Classification and Treatment, has a compassionate view towards those who serve as chaplains and vocalizes a need for such workers to be able to minister within protective guidelines to protect them from the occasional prejudices of officials and staff. "Unless the staff and inmates today regard the chaplain and his work with respect," he noted, "whether they personally participate in it or not, a great obstacle to achievement confronts the chaplain." Giving examples of what he means by such obstacles, from his own experience he related:

> Some of the 'old line' guards not only were outspokenly sarcastic regarding the motivations of the inmates who attended the services, but also introduced obstructive custodial precautions. I recall one institution in which I observed a custodial officer who not only did not remove his hat in the chapel but also interrupted the service by loudly paging inmates [to tell them they] had visitors (1973:85.83)

Philip Priestley pointed out that guards felt a need to see that chaplains "were put in their places; denied effective shares in the distribution of power and squeezed into conformist roles" (1980:10). Moore, a retired correction officer from Arizona explained why officers could grow into such attitudes. He records examples of religious personnel and activities at Arizona's State Prison:

> The visiting preachers came from Phoenix, Arizona. One Phoenix couple had an odd system of rotation. One Sunday the tall, lanky minister and his dumpy little wife would represent the Baptist Church; the following Sunday they would arrive in cap and bonnet and preach for the Salvation Army. A Mexican Minister from Tucson preached in Spanish for the Methodists. Sometimes a delegation of self ordained ministers, usually a family group affiliated with some little known sect, arrived to shout and yell and pray and beat their tambourines in a frenzy of religious fervor. Once, an all colored visitation descended on us and almost caused a riot. One lady preacher who played the guitar and sang hymns came several times but quit in disgust after discovering that "Fat man," a burly Negro, and a convert of hers, was in the snakes for committing sodomy on a white boy after the services during which she had converted him. The prison also had its own chaplain, but he must have been disillusioned about his prospects of saving many convict souls because his services were short and to the point and he was always in a hurry to get outside the walls again.

The officer describes at length the careful decorating of a "Saint Dismis" chapel by an Irish Catholic priest, a decorating which included "a handsomely fashioned brass chalice, burnished to shine like gold," so that

> Some member of the congregation must have thought it was the real thing, because one Sunday morning it was missing from the altar. Father Murphy, mad as a hornet, berated his flock with a good Irish lecture against theft. His appeal for the return of the chalice and his promise of forgiveness were to no avail for we learned afterwards that it had been quickly melted down and made into junk jewelry for sale to the visiting public in the studio (Moore, 1969:58-59).

Joseph Ragen, longtime warden at Stateville Prison in Illinois, shared Moore's opinion that chaplains are often naive. In his muscle-flexing, institutional/personal autobiography, he wrote:

> A chaplain with proper perspective realizes that custodial officers view a side of inmate life he never sees. He knows that guards may see the insincere inmate after he has been to church or Bible class, or just returned from an interview in which he gave his best song and dance to the chaplain. He realizes that guards may see the way the inmate acts, hear the way he talks, observe the various means he uses in getting out of work or acquiring something he is not supposed to have. In other words, officers are apt to see incarcerated men at their worst, whereas chaplains are apt to see them at their best. Unless chaplains keep reminding themselves of things as they actually are, they are liable to grow starry eyed and too idealistic to be of any practical help to those who really mean business about becoming rehabilitated (1962:312-313).

Octavio Ballesteros, an educator at a large Southwestern jail, agreed with Ragen's view that chaplains fail to see reality. He blamed their presumed naivete on socio-economic background and lack of proper church training. He wrote: "It is my theory that many Catholic priests and Protestant ministers have not been conditioned to relate to prisoners and therefore these clergymen do not derive much satisfaction ministering to lawbreakers. Many clergymen share the prevailing negative attitude of society concerning the lawbreakers" (1979:113). He cited a particular example of how such a middle-class indoctrination tends to create more harm than good in institutions:

> Because Reverend L. had developed a network of contacts in the criminal justice system, he was in a position to use his influence to effectively assist jail inmates. A word from Reverend L. in the right ear could go a long way in helping an inmate to obtain a probated sentence or an attentive reception in

a courtroom. It was unfortunate he did not devote his time to assist inmates from the different minority groups. He seemed to be more interested in aiding young Anglo-American jailees than in assisting all the jailees (1979:104-105).

Perceptions of the President's Commission

The 1967 President's Commission on Law Enforcement and Administration of Justice pointed to the problem of the socio-economic background of chaplains and equated the problem with geographic considerations. In its report, the commission declared:

> Religious services are characteristically weak where the chaplaincy staff is deficient. This frequently is the case in institutions at remote locations, especially where the State provides only enough funds for a part time chaplain. In these instances the institution often employs a chaplain whose primary commitment is to his outside congregation. He has little time for functions at the institution other than the weekly conduct of religious services. Also, such an appointee often is more oriented to a rural audience than to the predominantly urban institutional population; so he has difficulty in communicating effectively with the inmates. Where the institution is large, he may have a thousand or more inmates under his charge, far too many for much personal communication of any sort" (1967:53).

The President's Commission referred to the chaplain as "an appointee." This places focus on another recurring problem. Chaplaincy positions carry a stipend. This fact can attract individuals who simply want an extra pay check, or clergymen who are unable to maintain a position serving a congregation. If a clergyman can find an appointed position in an institution which expects little of him (and many institutions would by happy with clergymen who preferred to involve themselves minimally, and who, thus, would only minimally intrude upon institutional schedules) this position can be a monetary plum. Thus the cynical view of chaplains expressed by a warden at Chino Prison:

> Too often the average prison takes on as its chaplain some friend of the warden or of the political boss who gave him his job. Too often the man hired under such a system is a misfit in the church, a preacher who couldn't get along with people or hold a parish. Before we opened the institution at Chino we decided to get the very best chaplain we could find. We had to move fast, for word had gotten out that the position was open and we had many applicants. One man, a chaplain in a large county jail, was sure he was going to have the job. He went to every politician he could find. He never came near me, but sent others to intercede for him. I think the county jail wanted to get him out and thought it would be a nice way to do it (Scudder: 1952:31).

These varied and often negative reactions to the chaplaincy on the part of institutional personnel reflect not that these individuals are anti-religion, but that they feel that misguided religious activities can contribute to dangerous and chaotic conditions within facilities, and that the chaplaincy, made diverse in quality by the quality of the individual chaplains involved, can be considered a negative as well as a positive office in actual practice. The same divergence of opinion is manifest with respect to prisoners.

Chaplains as Seen by Inmates

There are many inmates who stand ready to attest to the good influence of institutional chaplains in their lives. Daniel Glaser refers to one ex-offender who "decided in prison that when a man like the chaplain could give up life on the outside to come inside a place like Leavenworth to try to help the kind of men they have there; there must be something to religion and he would accept it" (1964:145). The nineteenth century account *Prison Secrets* records a Quaker inmate at Ludlow Street Jail saying: "The doctrine of the chaplain mayn't be mine, but I tell thee, he brings the only sunlight that comes into this dark corner of iniquity" (MacDonald, 1893:38).

Throughout prison literature there is agreement that there is always a small percentage of inmates who have a solid religious background to begin with and who seek the solace of religion while imprisoned. A great majority of inmates, however, both in the past and present are seen to come from "unchurched" backrounds, often belonging nominally, at best, to a particular denomination. Their attitude toward chaplains oftentimes reflects a street wise, immediate practicality.

Christian tradition has rightfully made much of the criminal, dying next to Jesus, who, after asking him, "Remember me when you come into your kingdom," is assured, "This very day you will be with me in Paradise." Unnamed in the Gospel, he has been dubbed "Dismis." Churches and prison chapels have been named in his honor. Less emphasized is the crucified criminal on the other side of Jesus whose common sense street practicality limits his hopes to the manner of living he has known. His request: "If you are the messiah, then save yourself and save us." The kingdom of God is to be manipulated to his own advantage.

And why not? Such men are understandably desperate. In *Scottsboro Boy,* a wrongfully convicted and embittered young black man made an observation about inmate piety: "I studied how these guys came by their religion. They professed great feelings about God. They only pretended, the way it looked to me. They wanted any help they could get, to make it lighter for them. When you are drowning in the death row, the Bible is the straw you grab" (Patterson and Conrad, 1968:231). An inmate cited by Priestley in *Community of Scapegoats* notes:

> There are a lot of Bible punchers here. A lot of hypocrites. They go to all their services but it's only to get something for themselves from the people who come in from outside to run them. Singing hymns; I don't know what good that does them (Priestley, 1980:99).

In *The Angolite,* published by inmates at the off-shore, island-bound Louisiana State Prison located in the Gulf of Mexico, the problem of inmates who manipulate religion is addressed:

> The total involvement of religionists and organizations with the inmate and all of his problems has one drawback — one that everyone recognizes. It invites con and deception by insincere inmates hunting ways to secure their needs or obtain assistance in their efforts to regain their freedom. Outside religionists and organizations promising to become totally involved with the inmate and assisting him with all his problems create situation ripe for exploitation by criminal in insincere inmates. The only requirement is that they ride the religious pony and, given their basic criminality, deception comes easy (Rideau and Sinclair, 1981:49).

"All the Evangelists and religionists asked by *The Angolite* about the fakers," noted the editors, "admitted to having been stung and disappointed by someone they believed in who reverted back to crime after their release." Nevertheless, one of the institution's chaplains realistically responded to this charge with a shrug, saying:

> I don't care why they come. I feel that whatever their reasons are, if they come they are going to hear the Gospel, and they're not going to go back the same. My chief concern is that God spoke in the book of Matthew that, when he was in prison we didn't come to see about him. And further on, he breaks it down, letting us know that he means everybody who is in prison (Rideau and Sinclair, 1981:49).

An Encounter with Lemuel Smith

That chaplains are oftentimes easy marks for those inmates choosing to "ride the religious pony" was, in the recent past, brought home most forcibly to this writer. Convicted multiple murderer Lemuel Smith was incarcerated in the facility of which I am chaplain. Because of the bizarre nature of his murders, including the biting and dismembering of his victims, Smith was kept segregated in special housing.

I had a particularly personal problem in having to approach him. One of his victims, a clerk in a religious goods store, was the mother of a high school friend of mine. The motive for the killings had seemingly been the refusal of the store's proprietor to buy some religious pictures which Smith had drawn. When the bodies of the proprietor and the clerk were found, it was discovered that the clerk (my friend's mother) had been decapitated and her head placed in a toilet.

Whenever I visited Smith at his cell, he stared, unblinking, at me with his light gray, piercing eyes, telling me that his dead brother spoke to him "from inside himself" and "told him to do things." I did for him what I minimally had to do in order to salve my conscience that I was doing my job. I never told him that I knew his victim. Not very long afterwards, sentenced to Greenhaven Prison, Smith was given a job as a clerk by the Catholic chaplain. That he was the chaplain's assistant was brought out in the media after a woman correction officer was murdered, and her body, bearing bite marks, was found in the prison garbage dump. I was stunned as I read the accounts of the crime. It was beyond my imagination to conceive how, with his record and personal bearing, Smith could ever have gained such confidence from any chaplain in so short a time.

Faced with the fact that they are manipulated and used, many chaplains put up a defensive guard against being conned. Moreover, as government employees, "being part and parcel of the prison, they may become identified with it in the minds of the prisoners" (Klare, 1960:80). Thus, one finds a steady stream of inmate witnesses in prison literature who write off chaplains as being useless. Henri Charriere, in *Papillon*, wrote: "I trampled on the Catholic priests who heard the confessions and therefore knew what was going on in the bagne and said nothing" (1970). Jack Abbott, in *In the Belly of the Beast*, spat:

> The prison clergy, the easiest of all to intimidate, keep their mouths shut because (they whine) they cannot "prove" anything, and, you know, the evil

is outweighed by the "good" they can do if they just keep quiet and "do what they can." If they speak out they are fired (1981:121-122).

The Sorriest Job on the Farm

Philip Berrigan, a jailed, activist priest, attempted to maintain a network of meetings with his fellow advocacy-oriented prisoners and scornfully wrote of a fellow priest: "The Catholic chaplain wasn't open to this sort of thing; it was useless to approach him" (1970:52). In *The Prison Community*, Donald Clemmer, who is strongly negative in his assessment of the impact of religion and of chaplaincy in prison, quotes an inmate:

> Your prison parson daily comes in contact with men struggling to rise out of the mire of a past environment, but does he extend them a helping hand; does he interest himself to the extent of swaying the prison officials in favor of the convict who is trying to better himself? He does not. In an apologetic manner he will tell you, "I will see what I can do," a time worn expression of prison officials and there the matter drops. His job is political, and like all political appointees, he "passes the buck" (1958:236).

In Karl Weiss' *The Prison Experience*, another inmate says:

> This is not to say that the thirteen hundred men here at Rahway are without religious representation. To the contrary, Catholic and Protestant services are scheduled for every Sunday; Bible classes and religious tracts are available in abundance; religious medals and rosaries are yours for the asking. Salvation of the Spirit is the theme but little, if anything, is said of our Physical needs. Of what practical value is a Bible to me (except to roll cigarettes when I run out of cigarette paper) when I need someone from my home town to keep me informed about my ailing children? Or how can the Sermon on the Mount help a youngster who is on the verge of suicide and cannot find anyone to speak to who is in a position to help him? (1976:234).

In *Death Row*, an inmate attests: "The chaplain, he's about the sorriest bastard on the farm." Citing an instance wherein a man from the chaplain's own church was imprisoned and wondering about his sick father, the inmate records:

> For a week or two he said to the chaplain, "You know my mother. You've known her for ten or fifteen years. Would you call her and see what's happening to my Dad?"
>
> He said, "I can't do it."
>
> Now how would that hurt any TDC rule? Every time you talk to him he talks to the major. It's true. You can't tell him anything (Jackson and Christian, 1980:194).

John Godwin, in *Alcatraz: 1868-1963*, says of the chaplain: "The cons had their own way of assessing him . . . 'What's the new Bible pounder like? Does he whine at you? Does he bitch about the daddies and the queens? Above all — does he stool?" (1963:182). Similarly, Runyan, in *In For Life*, records the judgement of an inmate:

> The Protestant chaplain made a nuisance of himself for a while, but I solved that problem by pretending to be asleep. At first I was polite when he came down, so I would find myself standing first on one foot and then on the other while he talked about baseball and told me what an athlete he had been in his youth. If someone would listen he would spend hours on the same subjects. One of the fellows wanted to talk about religion, but he would have none of that — he wanted to talk about baseball. Evidently the Catholic chaplain felt we were poor prospects, for he only walked past once to tell each man hello. There was no going to church from Lockup, so if any of the fellows felt religious they must have done some considerable withering on the vine (1953:236).

Inmates on death rows, facing eternity, find little solace according to the testimony of some inmates held there. One such man, in an interview, said: "Okay, when the chaplain comes around, he — I mean, they almost make you want to — okay, like if you come in here believing in God, you most likely leave out not believing in God" (Johnson, 1981:167).

In a different book about death row, another inmate expands upon this portrait:

> Even the preacher here, he don't want to talk to you about God. He'd rather joke and clown around. I don't see him. He come in and be in the dayroom with us, and he won't talk. He'll talk to the religious guys, but if it get too far down into the religious he'll ease off. He'll light his pipe and he's off.
>
> (Interviewer: What does he talk about?)
>
> Bullshit. You know, just regular old stuff. Laughing and talking. Playing dominoes. That's what he's into. So I just don't bother him that much . . . The chaplain doesn't know nothing. You remember old Schultzy from "Hogan's Heroes"? I see nothing. I hear nothing. That's him . . . I asked him one day [if] I knew he was coming. I says,"Chaplain, if they take me to the death house will you go with me?" and he says "Yeah." I says, "Will you go with me when they take me to the stretcher?" And he says "Yeah." I says, "Will you go in my place?" I had him going and I threw that monkey wrench in there (Jackson and Christian, 1980:193).

The Bible in a Death Row Cell

In the brilliantly written *Star Wormwood*, Curtis Bok describes the death row reactions of a young murderer, raised without religion: "The Bible was the only object in his cell besides his bed and chair and table, and its unfamiliar words failed to interest him. He looked for stories of fights and battles in the Old Testament, but they didn't amount to much, and the Christian doctrine bewildered him" (1959:165). At the hour of execution, he pleaded to be able to visit with one last person who had come to see him, beyond the time allowed:

> Roger was in torment and poured it out to the chaplain when he came again, but the chaplain only shook his head mournfully and said there was nothing he could do.

Enmeshed in a system of rigid rules, the chaplain was in no position to do anything effective. At the last moment before the boy was taken to the death chamber, he played a mechanical role:

> At twelve twenty five they came for him. Well used to the routine, the chaplain rose and held out the cross to Roger, who convulsively grasped it and the chaplain's hand together, less in religious fervor than for support (1959:180-181).

The chaplain's role was as passive as if he had been a piece of flotsam grabbed by a drowning man in raging floodwaters. In *Prison Days and Nights*, inmates agree that the chaplain is worse than useless, a phony, profiting from their suffering:

> "And take the chaplain," says Number Four, "he's been here all his life. But what does he know? Only what them Goddam Bibleback cons tell him over in his office. He wanders around the shops and yard and says 'Hello, how's things,' and gives a speech in the chapel on Sundays. That's all he knows. But every other day you see a piece in the papers where he's giving a lecture to some club, or something, about 'Within Prison Walls.' Can you tie that? Why, he don't know what it's all about yet he never will know. But he gets paid for those lectures. What a racket he's got" (Nelson, 1933:211).

Mark Benney, in *Gaol Delivery*, attempts to balance matters by noting that the view of inmates with regards to chaplains is "both a dim and distorted impression." Yet, while reducing the weight of such complaints, he nonetheless decides, "the negative impression is strong enough":

> Nothing is clearer than the fact that, whatever else they are, our prison chaplains . . . are not bringing burning conviction and untiring energies to

bear upon their little world of separate cells. They are not assessing the system in the light of the Christian revelation and leaving no stones unturned until it conforms with their vision. At their best,they visit the lonely in their cells and bring a little comfort and sympathy. At their worst they sermonize (1948:39).

COUNTERPART VIEW: THE QUALITY OF INMATES' RELIGION

If the inmate view of chaplains is negative, one might be tempted to expand upon Benney's defense of a "distorted impression" and make a return judgement upon the critics, saying, "consider the source." The loaded cannon, pointed at the inmates in the yard during services at the Walnut Street Jail, may have been placed there at the result of a thoroughly rational reaction to a given situation. One considers the nineteenth century description (by an inmate) of the "hideous roars and general imprecations" of the prisoners which rent the air as soon as chapel services were completed at Ludlow Street Jail, as if the time of prayer had been too much for them to bear. Rev. John Clay wrote that "religious teaching in Gaols was a mere casting of pearls before swine; that drunkenness and promiscuous intercourse among the prisoners would have thwarted the most zealous chaplain" (1861:17).

Lionel Fox, in *The English Prison and Borstal Systems*, warns prospective chaplains of the phenomenon of "prison religion," which he defines as "the hypocritical approach which looks for some material advantage from playing up to the chaplain." He cites as an example the inmate seeking to receive the Sacrament of Confirmation (a sacrament which is received only one time). He balked at attending classes, saying, "Why chaplain, I don't need no preparation! I've been confirmed three times already" (1952:203).

The Rev. John Munro, a chaplain at New York's tombs at the turn of this century, gave his impression of the typical inmate, saying: "The fact is, he will not tell the truth even though in the end it might do him vastly more good than a lie." (1909:82) Donald Clemmer offered much the same opinion, saying: "It is the writer's impression that the majority of both Catholic and Protestant inmates are religiously insincere" (1958:238).

Drug-Dealers, Queens, Hostage-Takers in the Temple

Writing about women's institutions, Esther Heffernan observed: "Several of the women who asserted their dependence on religious faith refused to participate in the prison religious program because of its use by inmates for secondary ends, particularly the manipulation of religious personnel and utilization of services for purposes of play" (1972:141). Prison guard Daniel Moore described similar "play" in Arizona's State Prison:

> Many of the toughest characters inside the walls attended church, but not necessarily to get religion. Here they might make contact with a pusher to have a bundle of dope delivered to a certain spot at a designated time, or set up a tryst with one of the queens for a little quick loving in the showers or a broom closet. It was easy to spot the ones who had other things on their minds than the services. These always picked their seats near the characters they wanted to contact . . . A look over the congregation was not one guaranteed to bring sweet dreams. There were some of the hardest, ugliest and most repulsive looking faces one could imagine, and some of the men were plainly under the influence of drugs or marijuana. Even the guards were relieved when a service was over and the preachers safely escorted beyond the gates. One never knew when a plot to grab and hold ministers as hostages in an escape might erupt (1969:58).

In one of *Papillon's* escape descriptions, the attempt is planned to occur during Mass; a time when inmates from different areas of the prison are allowed to congregate, security is necessarily broken down, and the opportunity is ripe to take the priest as a hostage (Charrier, 1970). Commenting upon the "prison truism" which holds that "all rapos are Bible backs," Philip Priestley, in *Community of Scapegoats*, downplays the statement, but nevertheless agrees that there seems to be a consistent fascination with fundamentalist religion by inmates who have perpetrated crimes which would be held as particularly despicable in the judgement of society. The quest for religion becomes a quest for "certainty and predictability." Priestley quotes one such inmate who decided that " . . . with the Pentacostals you feel ashamed and you tell somebody about it and then you can go on from there. It's more definite and it comes from the scriptures . . . You know where you stand" (1980:97).

Redemption vs. Saturday Night Live

The notion of becoming "born again" to solve one's problems is a common phenomenon within prisons, and, like Fox's thrice-confirmed candidate, some recidivists even manage to become "born again . . . and again, and again . . . "

One inmate captured well the will-of-the-wisp nature of many prison religious experiences when he acknowledged: "The lady that I'm discussing religion with now, she told me to just forget about religion and try to get closer to God. Okay, you try that, but, like they say, it takes patience and time, but you don't have that. You've got the time, but you don't have the patience. You're supposed to meditate on God. Okay, you start meditating. I meditate for about five minutes and then I just get bored with it and I get up and start something" (Jackson and Christian, 1980:208).

Another inmate vented his feelings about the inmates who succeed in becoming "born again" for the duration of their prison stay:

> These people that are on the God trips get the TV turned on at nine in the morning so they can sit there and watch those crying evangelists. That right there is the most nauseous thing . . . I'm sitting there saying "Garbage, garbage, garbage." I got one each side and they stand at the bars with their hands in a praying position watching it and when they say, "Let's read," I can see their hands disappear. They're getting their Bible. They thumb, thumb, thumb through their Bible. I say, I hope this is helping them, 'cause it's making me sick. It's those ones that are like that that don't like "Saturday Night Live" because of the sex and all this kind of stuff (Jackson and Christian, 1980:209).

The Conversion Phenomenon

A pattern of conversion develops, differing from one geographic area to another. In an area where groups such as "The Full Gospel Businessman's Association" are known to take good material care, after release, of those who have been "born again" according to their particular rules of salvation, conversions will grow apace with such assistance. In areas where the Catholic Church has a good social service network, "knowledge of such comforts tends to encourage prisoners with no strong religious beliefs to embrace Catholicism — at least temporarily" (Smith, 1962:16).

Esther Heffernan points out that such a shift from one religion to another in prison "may well reflect the availability of differing secondary opportunities and institutional orientation on the part of

the two religious programs" (1972:141). Describing the same phenomenon, Rabbi Leibert uses the example of a regular member of
his prison choir who pressed the Rabbi for a parole recommendation
based upon his religious observance. Leibert hesitated, on the point
that the inmate was not Jewish. The inmate responded: "Look Rabbi,
I know I'm not a Hebrew, but a heathen. But the board doesn't give
a hoot about my conscience or my beliefs. All they're interested in is
whether or not I attend services. And that I do, as well you know —
or come your choir sings so sweetly?" (in Leibert with Kingsberg,
1965:88).

Kassebaum, Warner, and Wilner, in *Prison Treatment and Parole
Survival: An Empirical Assessment*, while describing a California institution, noted that "one of the chaplains estimated that about 25%
of the men attending services are 'shucking it,' that is, going to
church to impress the adult authority (parole board). This does not
appear to be undue cynicism" (1971:24).

Nor was it cynicism on the part of Father Eligius Weir, chaplain
at Stateville Prison for more than four decades, to decide that 95%
of the inmates leave after their time of incarceration "wiser but not
better men, wiser in the sense that thereafter they observe the
eleventh Commandment; Thou shalt not be caught" (Weir and Kalm,
1936:44).

Riding the Religious Pony

Weir's professionalism was praised by James Jacobs in his book
Stateville. Father Weir, he noted, "holds several advanced degrees
and is the author of a textbook on criminology. His recall of names,
facts and events going back almost fifty years is nothing short of
remarkable" (1977:249). In Father Weir's own book, *Crime and Religion: A Study of Criminological Facts and Problems*, the priest carefully
uses statistics to show the tendency of inmates to use religion for
secondary purposes.

Parole, in Illinois, was established in 1894. In that year the percentage of church-affiliated inmates at Joliet Prison, for all religions
put together, was 37.08%. This figure had remained fairly constant
for the fourteen years prior to 1894. In 1894 claimed affiliation
suddenly skyrocketed to 80.52%. In 1910 the figure exceeded 99%.
For the twenty three years prior to his writing in 1936, the average

was 96%. Weir wondered: "Had the underworld suddenly got religion?" When one Catholic warden at Joliet, John Whitman, began attending services with his wife and word got out that he and his wife helped men to find jobs after release, there was "a marked increase in attendance at mass." When Whitman left office, "the attendance at mass dwindled to almost nothing."

"Hence," Weir concluded, "the very pardonable effort of incoming prisoners to line up as many friends as possible, especially among charity and religious workers; in particular their effort to get the good will of the chaplain, the effort to appear as religious as might be, with much to lose and little to gain by assigning no religious affiliation" (1936:24.38).

This riding of the religious pony was included by Clemens Bartollas in his listing of a number of games which young offenders could play within institutions. He called it "the Theological game," and described a routine involving an initial con — impressing the chaplain with one's religious orientation; a routine to be played, going to the chaplain's office often, engaging his sympathy, requesting his intervention; and, finally, the payoff — convincing the chaplain to help gain the inmate's release (in Bartollas, Miller, and Dinitz, 1976:191). Given such observations it is little wonder that many chaplains gradually develop a jaded attitude about the religiosity of inmates.

Attitudes of Organized Religions toward Jail/Prison Clients

If the chaplaincy is of disputed value as a ministry as seen by some observers within institutions, its value is no less questioned by those outside of institutions — even by those within the ranks of organized religions. Jail educator Octavio Ballesteros opines that some clergymen would argue that sending a minister to a jail on a full-time basis is a waste of religious talent because

- most offenders probably will commit another felony upon their release,
- most jailees seldom attend church services in the free world,
- many jailees attempt to "con" ministers into doing special favors for the jailees which are non religious in nature (1979:113).

Such a judgement gives evidence of a view of social reality which has remained constant throughout all of history. Good people ("do-gooders") wish to do nice things for the downtrodden, but have no desire to diminish the social chasm which exists between contrasting segments of society, nor do they want the great mass of downtrodden to enter, as such, into their own, local, congregation of worshippers. In stark contrast to the founders of the world's great religions who lived among and embraced the outcasts of society, the descendants of these founders then keep themselves physically apart from the great unwashed.

In a chapter entitled "Church or Religion?" in his 1938 book *Invisible Stripes*, Sing Sing warden Lewis E. Lawes presents one of the finest indictments this writer has seen against mainline denominations and their aloofness from people who make up the underside of society. Lawes contends that churches like to score points by doing visible charities among the poor, but they do little to touch the lives of these people. "The fault is not with religion as an ideal, but with the church as an institution," Lawes insists, adding, "Faith is meaningless and vain when it is disassociated from social consciousness and group responsibility" (1938:253).

"Church Is For Nice People"

Lawes cites numerous inmates who are respectful of the churches which brush against but do not enter their lives: "I ain't askin' for no prayers at my funeral, Warden," one old man said, "They ain't got no prayers c'n fit old John" (1938:253). Another inmate remembered being sent as a child to beg coal from a church. The clergyman gave him the coal but threatened the boy with hellfire if he were begging it to sell it. The tattered youngster knew nothing of the theology of hell. Thus, the only effect of the lesson was: "I kept thinkin' how nice it would be in hell where you wouldn't have to worry about no coal in winter" (1938:255).

Another inmate remembered wandering into a church as a child and being thrown out by an usher who told him, "Get out, this is no place for loafers." When, in tears, he later told his mother of the incident at home she comforted him in words appropriate to their station in life. "The likes of you don't belong there," she said, "Church is only for nice people." Relating this to Lawes the inmate confessed, "I guess I'm still not nice people" (1938:266-267).

Lawes recounts with scorn the request of a clergyman wanting to witness an inmate's execution so that he could vividly use the man as an example in a sermon. With equal scorn he notes that he, himself, when speaking at churches drew great crowds because of his title of Warden at Sing Sing. Audiences who came expecting to hear war stories were invariably disappointed when he spoke, instead, about their own social responsibilities towards offenders.

Accusing churches of "bartering the homely virtues of charity and sympathy and brotherhood for the cold symbolism of form and ritual," he states that "the true 'defender of the faith' is he who can associate faith in the Divine with a sense of responsibility for fellow human beings." The truly appreciated clergyman, he insists, is one who will "descend from the eminence of his pulpit to implant words of cheer and comfort to the sorely tried in mind and soul" (1938:261, 270).

Lawes' picture of the dichotomy which exists between the world of respectable churchgoers and the world of disreputable inmates is reflective of the history of religious involvement in jails and prisons in the United States. Americans wanted to see themselves as a religious people, reforming sinners. Thus, those who were the "powers that be" in churches sat at table with the "powers that be" in the prison system to decide how to reclaim the incarcerated. But all such public relations imagery remained worlds away from the scrawly reality of facility tiers and the task of the chaplains who actually ventured onto them.

Butts and Barth on the Nature of Punishment

W. Marlin Butts of Oberlin College quotes the European theologian Karl Barth who, after visiting American prisons, noted the inhumanity of conditions in the United States as compared to prisons in his own country, where he customarily preached in prison chapels. Barth said: "The churches should be doing something about this." And yet, Butts says, the churches are not only not interested in what goes on behind prison walls, but have, as well, very little interest in accepting ex-offenders into their midst. "Even if we had excellent chaplains in all of our prisons and many men and women left prison with a desire to continue to be participating members of the church," he asks, "What are their chances?" Of the chaplaincy, Butts says, "I have never had a young man approach his denominational leadership without being asked, 'Why are you leaving the ministry?'":

> The result is that many of our prisons have chaplains who have been discarded by their denomination because no local parish wants them and they are committed to life as a chaplain in prison. This does not represent many of the younger men who have chosen the chaplaincy as their specialized ministry, nor many of the very devóted, capable men who are found throughout the country in state and federal prisons. But it represents an attitude of the church and accounts for a very inadequate staffing of far too many chaplain positions (1966:75-77).

Perceptions of the Inmates at Angola

The inmates at Angola Prison in Louisiana published a perceptive study of religion within their own facility which says much about religion in prisons in general. The dominant theme throughout their article is the portrayal of state employed chaplains and services provided by the mainline denominations, contrasted with inmates who joined quickly proliferating and short-lived fundamentalist groups from outside the facility. Of mainline representation, the inmates note that "the presence of religion, in most prisons, is just a token presence, like one chaplain" (Rideau and Sinclair, 1981:34).

Their own head chaplain, Rev. Joseph Wilson, who supervises a staff of three full-time and four part-time chaplains for a prison with 4200 inmates, notes that he could use 25 to 30 additional chaplains. Assistant Warden Peggi Gresham concurs with him, putting the desired number at 15, and qualifying, "I'm talking about good chaplains, top notch chaplains. But we can't. We don't have any positions authorized. We've asked for them repeatedly. But the requests were rejected. Religion in prison is not a priority in this state" (Rideau and Sinclair, 1981:35-36). Nor is it a priority with the mainline denominations. The inmate paper notes:

> Back in 1973 prisoners had to call upon then Governor Edwin Edwards to intervene with the Catholic Church to secure a Catholic chaplain for them. The situation with the churches has been such that it causes one to wonder what would happen if the Department of Corrections didn't actually "hire" chaplains to minister to the prisoners. Apparently, where the Christian spirit doesn't work, the dollar will (Rideau and Sinclair, 1981:38).

> Head chaplain Wilson, a Protestant, is more charitable toward the Catholic Church. "You have to take into consideration," he tries to explain, "that the Catholic Faith is not as evangelistic minded as some of the more fundamentalist ones. However, they are involved in some activities that have to do with

the betterment of prison life, and that is in the area of prison reform (Rideau and Sinclair, 1981:39).

Father Paul J. Henry, national coordinator of chaplain services for the U.S. Catholic Conference in Washington, D.C., takes up this defense, and notes that the bishops of the United States are continually taking stands on social issues. He notes, too, that an era of shrinking numbers of clergy adds another problem to the situation:

Many times the individual diocese will look at the personnel and many times they have just enough to serve their own parishes. The result is that the parish is responsible for the care of the institutions and that places an extra burden on them which, often times, that's difficult for them to understand [sic] because they really have not been geared primarily to deal with that institution within their jurisdiction (Rideau and Sinclair, 1981:39).

But the bottom line is that there is often a feeling on the part of inmates that they have been abandoned by the church. Said one: "I was born and raised a Catholic, but they cut me loose when I fell in prison. You know, it's like they've showed me what they think of me. What do I look like running behind a church that gonna cut me loose soon as I get in trouble and don't show no kind of interest in me? They can keep it" (Rideau and Sinclair, 1981:39).

The mainline Protestant churches come off no better. That inmate article notes that social workers and other professionals come to the prison "like flies after sugar . . . but seldom the church." Even with a prison located within "the famed Bible belt, where people are raised in the church, where the church is regarded as the haven of hope, mercy, compassion and salvation," the church "has traditionally kept convicts at arms length. Oh, they'll donate money, erect statutes, give Bibles and greeting cards, and offer prayers for the lost souls, but they rarely get personally involved with Angola. Instead, they keep their involvement at a distance and feed its imprisoned souls with a long handled spoon" (Rideau and Sinclair, 1981:37).

A Pattern of Inherent Conflicts

Elmer H. Johnson, writing specifically about conflicts experienced by prison chaplains, decided that "churches have attempted to serve two opposing purposes: comforting the underprivileged while accepting the established social structure, and challenging the inequities sustained by that structure" (1978:457). The resulting situation, in the opinion of Father Joseph Sedlak, chaplain at Indiana

State Prison, is one in which "The church acquiesces to society's ways of life and plays little theological and religious games to compensate for its lack of relevance to life's problems" (Griswold, Misenheimer, Powers, and Tromanhauser, 1970:134). Such churchly games are well exemplified in a chapter, fittingly entitled "Dignitaries," from Larry Cole's *Our Children's Keepers*, describing conditions inside America's juvenile prisons. During the 1960s, J. Martin Poland, dexecutive director of New York City's Youth Home, found himself at loggerheads with the administrators of religious charities. As is recorded in "Dignitaries:"

> Poland's regime was marked by constant confrontations with his board of directors and City Hall over his public cries for detention reform. The Youth House Board, selected by the Mayor from lists provided by the Federation of Jewish Philanthropies, Catholic Charities, and the Federation of Protestant Welfare Agencies, thought Poland's utterances put them in a bad position. They were constantly being forced to answer for the public charges of their own employee. The Board's main concern it appeared was for peace and paper progress (Cole, 1972:16).

Eventually, bled dry by disciplinary budget cuts, Poland was forced to resign.

One of the mainline denominations which places a great deal of emphasis upon pushing for a moratorium in the building of new prisons is the Quakers. There is an historical irony in this, for it was the Quakers who did so much to give birth to the modern American "Penitentiary" system. Other mainline denominations have now been quick to join in the modern day crusade against prison construction. However, it is a crusade which can be waged on a safe, theoretical level of protest. Philip Taft, in an article entitled "Religious Reformers Want to Proclaim Liberty to the Captives," observes this safe, political tone:

> The large and wealthy mainline denominations offer bold pronouncements on Criminal Justice almost yearly at their national meetings. They are on record against the death penalty; most have written detailed statements criticizing incarceration and living conditions in prisons. But that's often where it ends (1979:39-40).

A young activist is quoted, speaking of her own denomination, "The Presbyterian policy is radical, but its implementation is not." In short, says Taft, "The mainline Protestant Churches and the Catholic Church are often content to make policy statements."

The New York Bishops' Pastoral

In 1984, the New York State Catholic bishops issued a pastoral letter about criminal justice. Watching its issuance while working in the trenches of jail ministry, I felt rather like I was watching rockets flying overhead from an unseen launch site to an unseen target. Nothing said, or, more importantly, nothing subsequently done, had any effect on the day to day battle in the trenches where I exist. Nor was my viewpoint as a chaplain solicited in any individual or canvassed manner. In the mid-19th century, Rev. John Clay had written, "with regard to Episcopal favor, some time will elapse before the nature and, I am bold to say, the value, of such labors as ours will be taken into consideration" (1861:614). That time has yet to elapse.

There is a double irony in the lack of relationship between church dignitaries and chaplains. The public pronouncements of Church higher ups, along with the public interest generated by the deadly prison riots of recent years, have helped place justice concerns on the list of trendy causes espoused by religious-minded, professional activists. Such activists, especially when they are jailed after public protests, often make the chaplain one of their targets because he works within the system. Already existing beyond the fringe of normal ministry because he works in a reality which he does not endorse but which he accepts in order to reach those who are incarcerated, he is made a butt of scorn by protesters who treat him as if he had drawn up the blueprints for the entire system.

The former Josephite priest and peace activist Philip Berrigan published his denigration of the Catholic jail chaplain who would not or could not facilitate the continued meetings of Berrigan and his fellow activists when they were jailed following a political protest. One would like to have read the chaplain's side of this incident as well.

Chapter 4

THE VIEW FROM THE CHAPLAIN'S OFFICE

The response of one prison priest to Philip Berrigan's back-of-the-hand slap to chaplaincy was a return observation about professional protesters: "It must be great fun to run up and take a crap on City Hall steps," he commented, "when you don't have to go into the building to work everyday."

That remark was offered by a friend of mine whose job requires him to go into the maximum security facility at Comstock every day. It was made during a coffee break at a state level chaplains' conference, an occasion where such irreverent comments are commonplace. Listening to chaplains speak at such gatherings provides an opportunity to enter into their world and understand their ministry, not as viewed by outsiders, as in the earlier chapters, but by themselves. The canvassing of these chaplains in a survey, and the following presentation of the views which they share about various aspects their very special yet hidden ministry, provides much the same rare opportunity.

The voices of the chaplains in New York's state system and in the Federal prisons who participated in the empirical study are tabulated in the sterile tones of statistical analysis in Tables 4.1 through 4.4, appended to this chapter — which, by their very nature, fail to reveal the richness of their responses to "open-ended" questions. Throughout this chapter, *when reference is made to the "open-ended" voices of chaplains, the commentator is identified by a number in parentheses*, corresponding to the brief descriptions contained in Appendix III at the end of this volume.

Thus, both the statistical analyses and the responses of subjects to those open-ended questions reveal that chaplains in New York state and in the Federal system agree that their work isolates them from the religous main stream, but at the same time they agree that most of them are in this work because they freely chose it and find it satisfying. One chaplain described this choice as a liberation from the "myopic concerns of a congregation" (14), while another opined that he'd "rather face a jail riot than sit through a parish council meeting" (64). For some, working in a prison means working with a congregation devoid of hypocrisy. Offered one: "When someone asks me about prison ministry, having served twenty years in a parish, my first answer is, at least here the men know they are sinners and are constantly reminded of such" (5).

Nonetheless, the separation from the mainstream comes with its cost. While agreeing that "the government does not truly respect religious personnel and programs," the chaplain of a large metropolitan facility likewise time took aim at a second target, noting that the church "leaves us totally isolated; they would willingly visit the sick, but not the imprisoned" (60). Yet another chaplain, serving at a local jail where many of the prisoners were home town folk, buttressed this view, decrying the "lack of concern on the part of the clergy to visit or call after you have contacted them about an inmate who expressed a desire to talk to someone from his parish" (55; Note 1).

While neglect of the churches irks some chaplains, most save their fire for the lack or respect on the part of civil authorities for "religious personnel and programs."

THE CHAPLAIN AS A GOVERNMENT HIRELING

"I do not believe that a chaplain should be an employee of the state," said Rabbi Leibert, "For when he is in the pay of the state he is no longer a man of God, but only an institutionalized piece of clap trap" (in Liebert with Kingsberg, 1965:165).

Here the chaplain is caught squarely in the middle. In the eyes of inmates, as is noted by Clemens Bartollas, "the chaplain is considered part of the establishment because he serves on institutional release and other important decision-making committees" (in Bartollas, Miller, and Dinitz, 1976: 191).

Charles Cottle's *Sunrise* depicts a Protestant and a Catholic chaplain making their rounds together through "the hole," a punishment tier where all privileges are stripped away. He wrote: "Generally their trip was a failure; none of these men were impressed by a God who allowed such a world" (1968:19).

If paying a salary to religious ministers nettles purists with regard to separation of church and state, it is even more galling to the clergymen who, paid by the government, must minister under the thumb of the government. Barbara Stolz notes: "The values promulgated through ministry may often conflict with institutional, custodial goals, particularly where the actualization of these values means that those in prison ministry must confront those in prison leadership and the mechanisms through which institutional goals are achieved" (1978:17). Rabbi Leibert records the result of one such confrontation, when the Warden of the facility demanded, "Why did you violate regulations?" — then finally picked up a rule book and "literally hurled the unaccommodating manual at me while he blustered and threatened" (1965:154).

This chaplain/writer was reminded of the politics of chaplaincy after battling with a local machine judge about his disparate sentencing policies; a battle which won play on television news (in the same afternoon of work on the bench this judge had sentenced a youth of 16 with no previous adult record to one to three years in prison for purse snatching and, then, a fellow machine crony to mere probation for bilking elderly clients out of thousands of dollars). The Sheriff called me to his office for a two hour "discussion" on the realities of life.

> "You embarrassed me," he said. Machine politicians had quickly jumped upon him, asking (so he related to me): "Can't you control your own man?"
>
> "I'm not your man," I insisted, "I belong to the church."
>
> He wasn't impressed.

Michael Wolff, in *Prison*, observed a "dual loyalty — one to the church, another to the prison department — from which chaplains suffer" (1967:256). No matter how strongly chaplains see themselves as advocates, and no matter how wary administrators might be of them as loose cannons who are not quite under their control as are other employees, chaplains nonetheless work under the weight of knowing that if they can be hired they can be fired.

"No Right to Think"

Indeed, in this respect, as a Catholic priest, I am much freer than my fellow chaplains of other denominations. Smaller denominations are fairly autonomous, and clergy are hired, paid, and fired by local church trustees. The worldwide Catholic Church, more tightly structured in hierarchy, has the final say in moving clergy about, and, significantly, takes financial care of its clergy. Therefore, as a Catholic priest, I am in no way dependent upon my secular employers for my livelihood. More independent than Catholic clergy in many other respects, clergy of other denominations are, ironically, more dependent than we are upon a secular salary, and this, making them more vulnerable, places greater risk of governmental pressure placed upon them.

Beyond such degrees of distinction there remains a built in tension between jail/prison administrators and all chaplains who work in the system, but who are not quite totally under the control of the system. Ranging from Stateville Warden Joseph Ragen who wrote that chaplains were "starry eyed and too idealistic" (in Ragen and Finston, 1962:312), to the warden who hurled the book at Rabbi Leibert, to San Quentin Warden "Judge" Ames who told his chaplain, "You have no right to think, Sir" (Lamont, 1961:135), admininstrators have frequently made it known that they did not feel that the presence of chaplains to be a blessing.

Chaplains are ready to return the compliment in kind. If they have "no right to think" they, in turn, feel that some administrators have no ability to think. "There are poorly educated officials who have the power to make decisions," observed one (23). Another described "the politics of administration [and] lack of professionalism" by pointing to "a sheriff who is a high school dropout, but astute politician with no background in criminal justice" (64). One chaplain said it all by digging his pen through the survey paper while writing out as his comment the solitary word, "ADMINISTRATORS!!!" (60; Note 2).

Determined to make chaplaincy fit into a measurable programs model, many administrators inundate chaplains with forms to complete in triplicate while they labor in what is essentially a spiritual, confidential and non measurable ministry. Chaplains resent the artificial "make work."

"I want to minister to people, not paper," objected one, "but the paper work must be done first. At times I feel the administration cares more about the paper than the soul" (40). Another chaplain added "on many occasions the paperwork gets ridiculous. It merely keeps some idiot bureaucrats in a job. Most of the paperwork has no impact on the daily responsibilities of a chaplain but merely justifies the job of some central office person who has, moreover, never been inside a prison or has any functional knowledge of a prison" (32). One could sense more frustration and anger in the statements volunteered about this item than were focused on any other subject touched upon in the questionnaire having to do with personal working conditions. The chaplains ministering in the tightly organized Federal system ranked it as the highest potential stress factor confronting them (Note 3).

PREACHING ABOUT LOVE IN A PUNISHMENT SETTING

The longtime 19th century chaplain Rev. John Clay felt that his "mission of mercy," was "not in the right place amidst whips, cranks, tread wheels and other constraints of bodily pain" (1861:614). Present day chaplains agree that their own mission means "working in an evil environment" (41).

"There is not one element of redemption within a prison setting," said the chaplain just quoted, adding that the emphasis in such a setting is the "punishment and warehousing of people [with] very little possibility of inmates being given the opportunities to encounter their value system as that value system which came into conflict with society." As phrased by Father James Collins, addressing the Seventeenth Annual Conference on Correction: "It is difficult for a man to accept that God loves him when he is forced to contend with a life of rejection and scorn by those persons whom he sees in his life relationships." For religious prisoners "the problem is sometimes compounded by those who jeer." Collins notes:

> They are subjected to feelings of anxiety which are not known in the free society where men are free to pursue their convictions and beliefs without the constant harassment which prevails in a confined area such as institutionalization (Ward, 1972:128).

This constant jeering and harassment is directed not only at other inmates, but oftentimes at the chaplain as well. Walking the tiers, a chaplain becomes something of a barometer and a target of inmates' feelings towards his jailers, God, Church, the institution, and society in general. He is also the butt of inmate groups at war with a segment of society of which they see him as a representative.

With enough self-discipline of his or her own psyche, a chaplain should be able to accept all this well enough, with allowance made for the inmates' singular and collective frustrations. This chaplain has learned to tune out verbal abuse; to sit on a tier radiator, let them get it all off their chests, and let it go right through me. I have had more than one inmate spit on me: this is difficult to tune out: an inmate on the mental tier once threw a cup of urine in my face: this is extremely difficult to tune out.

"The transitory nature of the whole thing makes relationships ephemeral, shallow and unsatisfying," observed one chaplain, adding that the adage "'do your own time' as a basic philosophy is diametrically opposed to building Christian Community" (26) — or, for that matter, a community that would reflect the moral teachings of any faith group.

And yet, as with so many other problem areas chaplains show themselves to be aware of negative elements involved without allowing themselves to be defeated by them. They agreed upon the contradiction of the setting with their message. But as one chaplain offered: "The impossibility of some situations merely reflects the ongoing dialectic of doing the Lord's work. To function within the constraints of a correctional system and yet to retain a religious and professional integrity remains the core/critical element of our ministry" (30).

In other words, chaplains preach love in the midst of a punishment setting but they are not the punishers. When right thinking prevails, both they, and the inmates are aware of this (Note 4).

CORRECTIONS OFFICERS

"Our work is not seen as useful or necessary to other more pressing demands of the prison system, i.e., security" observed one chaplain (67). This would not matter if such an attitude had no effect upon working conditions, but as another chaplain noted, "When it is obvious that top management could care less, subordinates take this as their clue, [and] dealing with uncooperative staff, whether the warden/superintendent or the newest correctional officer, can make for frustration" (25; Note 5).

Corrections Officers (univerally referred to as "COs") and chaplains share one very strong commonality. They are the only personnel within facilities who routinely do their work on the tier areas (not counting the most invisible people in jails/prison, i.e., maintenance workers). Given the officers' literal role as "gatekeepers," effective ministry is directly dependent upon their cooperation. It should not be surprising that the strongest feeling expressed by chaplains about other personnel have to do with them. Michael Wolff, in *Prison*, had observed:

> Prison officers tend to look askance at the liberty of action allowed to chaplains, often, it seems to them, in defiance of regulations and in a manner that makes it difficult for the uniformed staff to maintain good order and discipline. These strictures put a strain on the relationship of a chaplain with the staff (1967:256).

As already quoted, Philip Priestley judged that officers have generally seen chaplains as outsiders and tried to ensure that they "were put in their place; denied effective shares in the distribution of power and squeezed into conformist roles" (1980:10).

Reacting to this "squeeze," one chaplain confessed that "dealing with correctional officers and their general lack of interest and cooperation is a major stress problem" (61). A second decided that "officers think clergy are dogooders (save a soul) interfering with their routine" (58). Officers with such an opinion can hinder chaplains by their ability to "create roadblocks by failing to open doors/classrooms, losing required paperwork such as gate passes, and failing to make religious programming announcements when required to do so" (25).

One respondent observed that "COs obviously object to my giving service to the men. This is especially true in areas like [the segregated punishment tier] where I am constantly reminded that I ought not do things for these men because most are in there for assaults on COs" (21).

Sadism among the Staff

The most adversarial statement came from a chaplain at a medium security Federal prison who saw as his enemies "bad COs who are verbally abusive." Taking an offensive stance he declared: "Sadistic prone staff bother me and I report them immediately and do everything possible to get them fired. Most important watch dog function of chaplains, I think" (39).

This author almost chose to omit the above statement, not because it is so adversarial, but because it presumes a power which few chaplains seem to possess. Such a "watch dog" policy would certainly create a strong and united reaction from officers as a group.

The worst single month this chaplain has ever lived followed an incident in which a CO, on the mental tier, forgetting that I was on the tier, grabbed an inmate by the neck of his shirt and punched his face several times. For the month's time that the incident was under investigation, intense pressure was put on me to back down from my statement; that I had seen what I had seen. During that period I was kept locked on various tiers for hours at a time, locked off other tiers, and directly threatened with physical harm by one officer.

Working in a corrections facility is not a job for any of the clergy who enjoy being constant professional protestors in the cause of social justice. A chaplain simply survives and does what he can. But the long range effect can be devastating with regard to his credibility to others, and to himself. Cottle quotes an inmate throwing this challenge at chaplains:

I think you're fakers. You preach God, and yet you know the situation here. There is no God; or, if there is, he's poorly represented. Why don't you stop these people from treating us like animals? Where were you when they were beating me yesterday? (1968:19).

And yet, one cannot make simplistic generalizations about officers any more than one can do so about chaplains. Corrections officers, like any other cross section of people, exhibit a wide gamut of personalities. To balance the extreme examples of officers who will read a newspaper while supervising religious services, or use this time to clip their nails, there are COs who will come up to receive the Eucharist along with the inmates, or turn to shake hands with an inmate during the "sign of peace." There are officers who will take time to seek out the chaplain and advise him to look in on a particular inmate who is depressed.

Occasionally, there is the ironic situation when a chaplain will have to ease the transition for a new CO who is too gentle, or overtly friendly, for his role as an officer. Recently, there was hired in our jail a young officer who wore a "Jesus loves you" button on his uniform. Who was I to tell him what was true; that this would not help him in dealing with inmates? I let him learn the hard way (perhaps wrongly). He became a butt of inmates' and other officers' jokes. After about a month the button disappeared. Gently, I tried to put the situation into perspective for him. My line of reasoning was an example of the sort of inner conflict which rips chaplains apart. On the streets I would have applauded him for wearing his faith out loud in such a way, but in jail the button only marked him for laughter. And yet, as I explained this to him, what was I saying about myself, and my own uptight, schizoid role?

Deepening Respect

There is a time element involved in the two examples I used from my own experience. The beating incident occurred in the 1970s when I was still green as a chaplain. I think that today I could handle such a situation by negotiating with the officers as a group rather than squaring off against them as if they and I were at war. The second incident, being able to sit down with a new officer to discuss, with him, the role he should play, came after years of experience and mellowing into my own role.

Other chaplains agreed about the seasoning of time. "I have a deeper respect for COs than when I started," (42) said one. Another concurred: "I am less judgmental about corrections officers, and see them as part of a team, whenever possible, working together" (4). A third posited that this team relationship was one which had to be carefully nurtured: "I've learned how to 'sell' myself to correctional personnel and not just insist that they must accept one simply by being a priest/chaplain" (30). No fewer than 14 of the chaplains, commenting as to how they knew when they were doing their job well cited feedback from officers and other staff members as a barometer of such. Such feedback was cited several times in conjunction with inmate approval — e.g., "when inmates and staff freely interact with me; with questions, dialogue and criticism" (42). It is an acknowledgment that, in the final analysis, every facility houses, for good or ill, a single community of human beings.

LIVING IN A WORLD OF REVERSED MORALITY

When the inmates in John Godwin's *Alcatraz* wonder if the new chaplain will "bitch about the daddies and queens (1963:182), " it is a reminder that a facility chaplain moves into a whole different moral world than he would know in a parish. It is a world whose moral perimeters are decided by inmates (Note 6).

It is distressful to minister in a world in which inmates prey upon one another, often to substitute for sexual activities which have been denied to them. It is more than just being forced to condone, by silence, activities which are considered immoral. The chaplain must live with knowing that he can do nothing to protect weak inmates from the strong. They know this and he knows it. Occasionally a new inmate will appeal to the chaplain to use his position to fight against homosexual activity and the threat of rape, to fight against kangaroo courts and blanket parties (the kiddie tier custom of greeting uninitiated new inmates by throwing a blanket over their heads and beating them senseless). When an appeal is made to the chaplain to "do something" about all this, it only adds to a sense of his uselessness in the eyes of the inmate, and, stressfully, in the chaplain's own eyes.

To prevent the inhuman activities of humans caged together like animals in a zoo, one would need to effect the total, constant separation of inmates into constant isolation, or hire as many COs as there are inmates. To seek the prevention of such activities is to seek the impossible. Nonetheless, it can make for a terrible feeling within oneself while working in such institutions as a ministry.

It is likewise stressful to be caught between what is right and wrong from a moral point of view, and with having to deal with sick individuals (Note 7). At the time of this writing, this chaplain is dealing with two teenagers who tied up an elderly woman in a rutal town, hacked her to death, and took her car. When caught, one of them was wearing the dead woman's wedding ring. Esconced in the jail's mental tier, this youngster, who blithely informed me that he is a "born again Christian," is trying to decide which of two girls to marry while he awaits trial. It might be the girl he "really" loves, or it might be the girl who is currently pregnant with his child.

At the age of 17, he has already sired two children by two former girl friends. Dare I breath a moral comment as I listen to this, or because he has already tried to hang himself twice and doesn't take too well to criticism, do I just sit on the radiator outside his cell and nod agreeably while he spills his guts? I do the latter. A fundamentalist such as the Reverend Jimmy Swaggart, who, on national television, has heaped scorn on psychology in the name of God, would apparently suggest a strong moralistic stand. For the chaplain who is struggling to do the right thing at the given moment, such a conflict creates a "no win" dilemma. Rabbi Leibert recounts an incident where he spoke with an individual not unlike the Lothario/murderer just described. He wrote:

As I listened to these outpourings, it occurred to me that the old term "desparado" in its original meaning of "desperate" was an apt description of the malum per se criminal. What could I do for such men? They needed individualized psychiatric care, creative and constructive outlets in an atmosphere that was therapeutic, not punitive (1965:140).

And yet, in another place in his book Leibert decides that the chaplain loses whether he chooses the route of professional counselling or of moralizing. "In my opinion," he wrote, "formalized religion is a dubious factor in therapy, especially under present conditions. Sponsored by the prison authorities, it is generally identified with them. Moralizing falls on deaf ears" (1965:24).

Many of the chaplains in this present study stood in agreement with this. One of them observed:

Many prisoners, from my experience, are amoral, not immoral. Most come from broken homes, had abusive parents, or lived in such poverty of soul and body that what they know is, in their own jargon, the "street ideas and realities." To them "the streets" are jungles. You feed on weakness as strong animals feed on the weaker. Crime, for them, is not anti-social but an avenue of obtaining what others have through opportunity, work or position in life (35).

Another concurred:

It seems that these men have been punished for wrongdoing so much that they no longer (if they ever did) see it as a corrective measure. Rather, it is accepted and even expected. Somehow punishment confirms who they are. It reinforces their worthlessness (13).

One chaplain who expanded upon the problem of "reacting emotionally against the dislikeable personalities of some inmates," observed that "some [inmates] are so compulsive and demanding of service and time I feel I am their father they never had — they act like 8-10 year olds, undisciplined and egocentric. The more you give, the more they want" (45; Note 8).

It is interesting that this complaint about the unreasonableness of inmate demands is placed, even when it is cited as stressful, in a contextual framework. The chaplain who is speaking serves at a maximum security prison. Yet, he is willing to write off the infantile selfishness of the inmates because of the limitations of the setting in which he is relating to them.

PROFESSIONAL STAFF AND CHAPLAINS

Conflict between chaplains and the professional medical-social worker-psychological staff is almost always assumed whenever the relationship is touched upon in criminal justice literature. In a chapter entitled "Prevention through Religion," George Powers builds a case that religion has no effect on prevention or rehabilitation until it enters into a secular realm to use secular tools such as psychology, and concludes that "isolationalism, denominationalism, and supernaturalism remove the church from its purpose of existence" (1967:125).

As guilty as the clergy may or may not be of "supernaturalism", the other side of the point made is that many professionals brush off religious personnel when they remain in their most proper realm, preaching religious values. In April 1987, a young man who had constantly been in and out of jail for alcohol-influenced minor disorderly conduct offenses was arrested again for throwing road signs into the Hudson River. He hanged himself while being kept overnight in a police lock up. I had once gone to an Albany judge to plead that he had severe problems and needed to be in a program.

The judge cut me off in midsentence to declare, "Aristotle, Father, said that the man who drinks and commits a crime should be punished twice; once for drinking and once for committing the crime." I subsequently wondered if that judge would have given me a better hearing if I had presented myself as a professional counselor rather than a man of religion. Professionals are quick to write us off as do-gooders. It gives one a sense of impotency. And yet, in this case, a life was at stake.

Brush-Off for a Nun

One day I witnessed a probation officer attempting to brush away a nun who was insisting that a particular teenager needed to be sent to a drug rehabilitation instead of jail.

"Now, Sister," he chided, as they stood in the main hallway of the Albany County Jail, "what are your credentials for deciding that?"

"I have a Ph.D. in counseling," she countered, "What are your credentials for questioning my credentials?"

The probation officer's blush colorfully underscored his unspoken answer that whatever level of education he had attained did not match her full house. The day after witnessing that scene I sent in an application to go back to school. If the "big boys" refuse to respect religious personnel in our proper role, it becomes a challenge to counter them in their own realm.

Much of the literature seems to assume that the quality of the chaplain is a variable (owing to personality, professional training, or theological outlook) while the quality of the professional staff is a constant. Not only are most professional staff members in correctional facilities overwhelmed by the sheer numbers of clients they must deal with, as individuals they are as variable in quality as any chaplains. While some chaplains worry about the professional staff's "lack of understanding of chaplain's role; that they see the chaplain "as just another counselor, specializing in 'bad news'" (49), others aggressively point to the bureaucratic weakness of the so-called "professionals." A woman ministering as a chaplain in a large county jail decried "staff inability, refusal, to make minor decisions, [and the] weakness and lack of leadership at top of staff where you finally have to arrive if you want some small decision to be made. Staff members fear being held to blame if something causes friction" (66).

Political Establishments and "Machines"

In a county operated by an entrenched, long-running political machine, this chaplain once worked in a jail in which a politically-appointed psychiatrist, while sitting in judgement over the mental capacity of inmates, had been, over the space of several years, been convicted of two DWIs; of assaulting a woman in a bar; and of a hit-and-run accident in which he struck a cerebral palsy victim in a wheelchair. Throughout all of this, the man held onto his politically powerful position and was instrumental in sending men and women to prison for crimes of which he was equally guilty.

In county jails, any psychological work done with inmates is often limited to a cursory judgement as to whether an inmate is capable of standing trial, or to see if an inmate should be housed in the jail's "mental tier." Beyond this, no real help is available no matter how mentally ill the inmates may be. In many urban areas, jail tiers for inmates removed from the general population because of mental problems become nothing more than places for storing sick people for whom nothing is being done except for over-medication. In these circumstances the chaplain walking the tiers must come to accept the fact that many people in dire need of help will not receive it. He must also listen to a constant litany of angry complaints about matters beyond his ability to rectify. The chaplain is, most often, a person who is not medically trained and has no way to distinguish those who are truly ill from those who perceive a headache to be a life threatening situation, or from those who, knowing the world of prescription drugs, are expert at concocting complaints to get such prescriptions. It is a matter of hearing the cry of wolf day in and day out, and of torturing oneself, wondering when the cry is real.

The chaplain cannot always turn for help to the politically appointed medical personnel with the presumption that they are dedicated to their patients. During one week in the fall of 1986, this chaplain began to notice that the inmates on the mental tier were "acting out" more than was usual. After two days of this an inmate on the tier dove off his cot, smashing his head against the opposite wall. At length, because I was pressing the matter, a nurse told me, "off the record," that the doctor was refusing to renew prescriptions until the county agreed to a pay raise he was demanding.

The professionals are not always professional, and this can aggravate an already uncomfortable relationship between them and chaplains. Removing himself from the lists altogether, one chaplain declared that he had "never seen it desirable to become close to staff. It is very difficult 'to live' in the midst of very divided factions" (26). In contrast to this, one reflective minister serving at a medium security state prison took a compassionate look at all of us who labor within facilities side by side (but not necessarily together) and suggested that we suffer from a failure to communicate:

> Often it seems that staff does not work in unity with each other toward the overall goal. There is little gathering of colleagues (chaplain/program people/security) to discuss problems. There has been no time when we gathered to set positive goals, develop an overall strategy, as a theme by which to improve the tone (atmosphere) of the institution. The goal (unspoken) seems to be: — "leave it alone" (13).

It is this lack of communication which is the basis of much of the conflict which exists between chaplains, administrators, staff, and corrections officers.

DEALING WITH SIMPLISTIC PUBLIC ATTITUDES

Demogogic politicians rend the air each election year with inflammatory rhetoric about spiraling crime rates and how they intend to control it by stiffer sentences and by filling the landscape with ever greater numbers of prisons. They know what they are doing. It gets them votes from people who think that there are easy and automatic solutions to societal problems.

"People outside don't care and have the misconception that the criminal justice system serves them or does some good for society" (62), said a chaplain at a large metropolitan jail, referring to simplistic public attitudes. Another chaplain joined him, calling the issue of public stigmatization of offenders "the worst by far" (18; Note 9).

"The mind of the public," offered a priest who serves in a maximum security facility, "is one that all criminals are bad and can never change" (34).

A Rabbi, expressing distress at "the realization that public attitudes will not change," personalized the issue by adding, "people fail to understand that what you do can also make a difference" (56). For him, the public's rejection of offenders logically involves a degradation of chaplains as well. Clergy, it would seem, who might better be serving Godly people in a congregation are wasting time and energy on criminals when it would be better to simply "lock 'em up and throw away the key."

Discounting the Chaplaincy

There is an ironic discounting of chaplaincy at the opposite end of the spectrum of simplistic public attitudes. This would involve activists who want to reform the criminal justice system in an overnight process and who show little patience with those working within it.

In *Prison as Political Institutions*, Barbara Ann Stolz wrote that "it seems extremely important that individuals working in a prison ministry continue to be able to share experiences with others involved with prisons; with other chaplains, reformers, volunteers, and those in social work, not just prison officials." Yet, she also acknowledges that chaplains cannot readily pursue such a program of information exchange, because "at times, the objectives of those in social ministry and even the official policy statements of the

Churches have been interpreted as conflicting with the goals and concerns of those in traditional prison ministry " (1978:18-19).

That statement points to an area of possible conflict for chaplains who would want to think of themselves as socially progressive but who are locked into that "traditional prison ministry" with all resultant ramifications. And sometimes it is the reformers who become desensitized to other views of thought by their own posture of protest.

Within recent history in Albany County Jail, at a time when the jail was already filled beyond capacity, overcrowding was heightened when a large group professional protesters, much like those whose above spokesman was Philip Berrigan, were incarcerated for a week after having blocked rush hour traffic at a major intersection in order to express opposition to United States' Central American policies. During their stay I became an object of their ire for "doing nothing" about the overcrowding of the facility. What I could do beyond organizing a jail break I didn't know, so I took their heat in silence. However, I must, guiltily, admit that I enjoyed in silence a sequence of events which occurred when the heat they gave so freely was turned back upon themselves.

After the protestors were released they called a press conference and opened fire on conditions at the jail. Their spokeswoman issued a blanket statement claiming that "the guards treat prisoners like things instead of humans." This lumped decent officers together with those who might properly be labelled hacks, and one officer who felt he did not deserve such a lumping decided to invite the spokeswoman (and the group) to put up or shut up.

Before departing her tier the woman had given the group's telephone number to an inmate and encouraged her to pass it along to anyone else who wanted to contact the group about matters at the jail. The offended officer, stumbling upon the number, made scores of copies and taped it over every tier end telephone in the facility, headlined with the invitation: "NEED HELP??? CALL..."

Within 24 hours, a tape machine was answering at that number. Within two more days, the group had a new phone number. It was an unlisted number. In that short time, they had had a taste of dealing with the avalanche of unsolvable human problems which those who work inside of the system must deal with every day.

Accepting the Confining Realities

This is not meant to minimize the importance of reformers and social activists. They are needed to keep a necessary political balance in this world, and they are needed as watchdogs who keep those of us working within the system from becoming complacent. But they must also be sensitive to the realization that those of us who work with the imprisoned deal with a reality which is limiting and that we cannot always march in step with them. Rabbi Leibert experienced this frustrating limitation when he disappointed a fellow rabbi, a social activist, by refusing to join in the movement to free Morton Sobell, convicted as a communist spy and serving time in the prison where Leibert was chaplain. Wrote Leibert:

> I would not have minded being in the company of such an eminent Rabbi as Rabbi Feidleman of New Orleans. But his situation and mine are not the same. I want to be Morton's spiritual mentor, and I might have jeopardized this service by signing or attending . . . In this I differed with colleague, the Protestant chaplain at Alcatraz, Rev. Peter McCormack. Convinced that Morton Sobell was the innocent victim of mass hysteria, he took an active part in the movement to free him only to find himself constrained to relinquish his ministrations at Alcatraz. (1965:47).

While political protestors have the luxury of first making a judgment in theory about what should be called just and then crying out about this judgment, chaplains, even when agreeing with them in theory, must accept the confining realities of working within the system which employs them.

RELIGIOUS COMPETITION

Kenneth LaMott's *Chronicles of San Quentin* refers to an era in which a state of "guerilla warfare" existed between Protestant and Catholic chaplains (1961). Such relationships existed as a reflection of the noncommunicating and competing stance of these two groups of Christians. George L Murphy, in his 1956 doctoral dissertation *The Social Role of the Prison Chaplain*, spends most of his study making comparisons between Catholic and Protestant chaplains which are now anachronistic, and which, even for that era, seem open to much subjective speculating (e.g., asking wardens how they rate different denomination chaplains as to their satisfaction with prison work; asking which denomination's chaplains were most effective in gaining the confidence of inmates, with helping them to reform, and with helping them adjust to prison routine).

Since the early 1960s, the Ecumenical movement which has been a deep and hopefully irreversible trend among the worlds faith groups, has totally changed this perspective. Chaplains representing mainline denominations tend to work together now within facilities, reflecting the growing harmony among religious faiths in the larger community. Interfaith frictions can still arise even in an ecumenical age, and in a facility these can be acerbated by shoulder-to-shoulder working conditions.

The Pivots for Competition

However, the survey comments made by chaplains — as well as comments made during the follow up phone calls after the mailing of the survey, such as that by a chaplain who told me not to bother contacting his fellow chaplain because "He's an old man who comes in once a week and sits around drinking tea" — would indicate that frictions generally arise not from religious causes but, rather, from complaints of an "office worker type." Characterisitc of such is the complaint of the respondent who cited "the cutting of corners and shirking of responsibility by some fellow chaplains" (61; Note 10).

Professional cooperation between mainline Christian churches, however, accentuates a division which has always existed within the wide spectrum of Protestant denominations, and which now exists with Protestants and Catholics on one side, representing denominations willing to mix religion with the sciences, and fundamentalist denominations on the other side, in general relying only upon the Bible as a guide to living and scorning any sort of wedding between professionalism and religion.

"We don't have high salaries, psychiatrists, government waste, records, secretaries and tomfoolery," said the Reverend Lester Roloff, at war with the State of Texas about his denomination's sole use of Bible exhortation in dealing with youthful offenders. Incensed at any idea of government control, he claimed: "It's the role of the Church to regulate the state, not the state to regulate the Church" (Corey, 1979:24).

In Philip Taft's article "Whatever Happened to that Old Time Prison Chaplain," an Evangelical minister at the Leavenworth Federal Penitentiary is quoted: "I'm open to anything that will help the men. But if it leaves God out, then it becomes the golden calf. We can all fall prey to the gods of psychotherapy, reality therapy, all kinds of stuff" (1978:57). The division between the fundamentalists and the mainline denominations is strongly felt, not only because of differing attitudes towards professionals in the field but because of differing attitudes about religion. "There is no love lost between them," notes Taft of the two groups.

The mainline denominations are preferable to prison and jail administrators because they work more easily within the structure of the system, and do not emphasize overt proselytizing. They serve those inmates who want religion, and serve them by the staid methods of the mainline churches within the community at large. In the view of the fundamentalists these denominations have sold out, becoming one with the societal golden calf. Fundamentalists, exemplified in the 1990s by the cable television evangelistic ministries, place a high importance on an emotional conversion, a "born again" experience.

Although they purport to teach only from the Bible, the fundamentalists put out volumes of conversion/witness books and tracts with a contrasting theme of salvation in Jesus or else damnation. These books (with sample titles such as *Go Tell It to the Mafia* and *I Was Bonnie and Clyde's Hit Man*) follow a non-varying plot pattern which this chaplain/writer has come to call "Jesus-came-to-my-cell literature." The main character has got to be bad. Real bad. And part of his being real bad is that he has been raised in a flabby, do nothing, mainline church. Then when all is at its absolute worst, the hero discovers the Lord in his cell. Not only does he get saved unto eternity, his zits get cleared up, his teeth get straightened, his hair gets fluffed out — the books, like weight reducing ads, include before and after pictures — whereupon he gets paroled, gets a four hundred dollar suit, and goes on the lecture circuit.

The Literature of Damnation

The darker, threatening side of this literature is evidenced in a typical tract, *All My Friends Are Dead*, by Reverend Freddie Gage. The title of his work refers to a number of people Gage had known who did not listen to his preaching and who are now forever damned. These include his grandfather (1986:23), a loving but irreligious man ("I watched him die without God and slip into Hell for all eternity."); a boy whose mother the Evangelist consoled at his funeral with the words (1986:20), "He didn't have to go to Hell, Mrs. Southerland. He chose to go to Hell. He chose sin, sex, drugs and alcohol. He chose to go with the Devil instead of Jesus." And there is his own drug addicted cousin (1986:20): "I preached my cousin's funeral. His little boy cried all the way to the cemetery and all the way home. He kept saying, 'My Daddy went to Hell.' That boy later developed emotional problems because of that experience. But the tragic truth in all of this is that my cousin chose to go to Hell" (1986:21). It never seemed to occur to the author that the boy's emotional problems might have had something to do with the funeral sermon he had preached.

This sort of colorful literature, along with the experience of declaring oneself "born again," is extremely popular with inmates who run on high emotions. Others often react strongly against the fundamentalist approach. Reverend Robert Rested, Jr., a Lutheran chaplain at a California prison, expressed disdain for their propensity to blast their way through a facility and then "leave to tell war stories about the men" (Taft, 1978:57).

The chasm between the mainline and fundamentalist camps also involves a question of turf. Official chaplains resent the free lancing, usually volunteer, fundamentalist groups (characterized by one mainline denomination chaplain in Taft's article as "religious nuts"), who, as Taft notes, make "inroads into their territory."

Volunteer Groups

It is in dealing with volunteer groups pounding at the prison door — crying out "the age old argument that if one religious group can do it, why can't we?" (44) — that the issue becomes a matter of religious philosophy for chaplains. Rating the issue relatively low as a stress factor, the chaplains contributing to the study nonetheless added sharply worded additional comments about the "fundamentalist views of volunteers" (4). One chaplain complained that "Proselytism by volunteers and the chaplain's clerk is a trouble," adding that such activities "foment hate and not love and fraternity. Worst problem in the work" (18).

Another concluded that "volunteer groups are a real problem when one thinks in terms of a consistent, growth producing, overall religious program" (5). The specifics of this "problem" were explained by another chaplain as "dealing with the absolute demands of religious zealots; fundamentalists fail often to realize the compromise of having to live in a multi-religious, multi-cultural setting. Their worship, dietary, or holyday observance demands often have no bearing on the needs of others" (42).

However, spirited, outside-the-system evangelists can sometimes act as spoilers, forcing chaplains to get moving and compete — if official chaplains are wed to the system and oftentimes mired in bureaucracy; if, as Taft notes, "even the best chaplain, it seems, reaches few men"; if, as prison officials agree, no more than 15% of inmates participate in religious programs, with only 5% of them "committed" to a faith (1978:55).

Former Nixon aide (and Watergate convict) Charles Colson has given ample proof that his book *Born Again* depicts no short-term, fading conversion. For years he has conducted his "Prison ministries," preaching in facilities and becoming a strong advocate of accepting the rehabilitated offender back into the larger community. Colson's "Chaplain Ray's" Texas-based "International Prison Ministry" publishes a large number of the conversion tracts mentioned earlier.

Beyond this, his well-funded organization promptly mails a Bible to any inmate who writes to him requesting one. If an inmate seeks a correspondence with his ministry the correspondence is kept up and conveys a strong personal touch. His "Prison Evangelism" magazine prints inmates' reflections and poetry, offering at all times an optimistic theme of success through God's grace. Forgetting philosophical differences, one is inclined to say, if it is a positive force in some inmates' lives, then, for them, it is a good thing.

Even beyond the invasion by outside evangelist groups, chaplains have to deal with inmate led religions. Just as jail house lawyers surface within facilities, so too do jail house preachers. Nor can they automatically be categorized with the type of inmates who created "The Church of the New Song" (CONS). Some prisoners, responding to the Biblical assurance, "Where two or three are gathered in my name, there also am I," eschew chapel services and gather in their own small communities.

The *Angolite* study of prison religion notes one such group at Angola: "the fifty six member inmate Church of God in Christ, led by an inmate preacher serving a thirty nine year sentence for robbing a Delhi, Louisiana Bank" (1981:32).

Do-It-Yourself Religion

In one sense, this do-it-yourself category poses no threat to a chaplain. If inmates genuinely interested in religion are a minority to begin with, such inmate groupings, a minority of a minority, able to meet only informally during recreation periods and unable to offer any of the social and legal advantages of "riding the religious pony," can be written off as, at worst, negligible. Nevertheless, to the chaplain who is sensitive to his own personal limitations and the necessary limitations of working in a state blessed ministry, such groups can represent an indictment of personal failure (Note 11).

Such conflicts all occur within the sphere of the United States' dominant faith group, Christianity. In the relationships between other major religions, there is generally little conflict between Christian and Jewish chaplains unless a matter of personality conflict is involved. This, quite simply, is a result of the fact that such chaplains are not in direct competition. In smaller institutions where the presence of Jewish inmates might be sporadic, a Christian chaplain is often the one that the inmate will approach, simply because such a clergyman speaks the language of religion and understands the Jewish inmate's needs. The chaplain then becomes the contact person between the inmate and a Rabbi from an area congregation.

In other respects one would make no distinction between the stress factors which face a Christian or Jewish chaplain. The frustrations which Rabbi Leibert (1965) records in his memoirs on the chaplaincy (dealing with authorities, inmates, outside pressures, etc.) might have been written by a minister or priest.

The increasing presence of Islamic Imams, on the other hand, brings a whole new dimension to the chaplaincy scene. These clergy are, situationally and comparatively speaking, so new as to be ignored in all but the most recent literature. They are not even mentioned in the 1956 dissertation by George Murphy, though Muslims at that time were a growing force in the prison system.

An Imam, seeking to establish himself in prisons and jails in this country, is often in the same situation which Roman Catholic priests faced in the midst of the 19th century's Nativist era. Facility by facility, they generally have to fight for their right to gain entry. Many administrators, hardened by incidents involving racist groups who unite, giving lip service to Islam, are reluctant to accept the possibility that some inmates have sincerely adopted the Islamic faith.

Once inside, Imams face a far sharper problem than Christian chaplains who must deal with tier congregations conducted by inmate preachers. Islam, in this country, developed largely from a prison movement which was parented by anti-white feelings on the part of black inmates. Nonetheless, just as entire peoples were converted to Christianity by conquest (e.g., Latin American Indians) or enslavement (in the United States) and subsequent generations of these peoples became Christian in fact, so too, a true Islamic faith has grown out of the first generations of protest conversions. This history creates no little problem for the Imam who enters a facility and has to deal with home grown philosophies which wear the name of Islam. An Imam has to differentiate true Islamics from jail formed groups who preach death to all whites. Imams also have to deal with officers, staff and other chaplains whose impressions of the still new rise of Islam are often clouded by negative experiences with racist groups.

Religion and Racism

For black Christian chaplains, these racist groups create potential stress because they are forcefully vocal in their ridicule of ministers who, they claim, have bought a "white man's religion." Such inmates will come to Christian services for the express purpose of destroying an atmosphere of worship. Moreover, in county jails close to the inmates' homes, the ministers oftentimes must deal with the division and sadness which this creates in families within his own community.

For white clergymen working on tiers these young "Five Percenters," as they call themselves, can be a constant source of stress. They become a target of anger (this writer/chaplain is accustomed to being called "the blue eyed white devil"). Their ongoing game is to gather in groups, follow the chaplain along the tier, and shout him down with derision so as to make conversation with any inmate on the tier nearly impossible. It is little wonder that it is not always easy for a chaplain who has been enduring this for any length of time to emotionally welcome the newly appearing Imams with open arms.

Anyone who has read accounts of facility uprisings in the United States in recent decades would be aware of the racial tensions which exist in prisons and jails. The item "Racial/religious tensions" hit home to chaplains in the survey; several worried about "the tensions between blacks and non-black inmates" (46). Others spoke of the racial posturing of some religionists: "Some pseudo-Muslim (Five-percenter) teachings by their chaplain — hostile to whites, harmful to young Blacks" (66). "Muslims are never satisfied and never grateful," groused one respondent (33). In assessing these views, however, one must keep in mind that the respondents to the survey reflecting the makeup of chaplaincy in general — were mostly white (91.4%) and Christian (85.7%). Islamic Imam, who are fairly new to the prison system and few in number, have to deal with ignorance about their role and their religion on the part of others, and have to deal, as well, with the reality that Islam, in the United States, has grown within the context of racial anger (Note 12).

It must be posited that this issue, to be fully discussed, would require a further, more extensive study focusing on Islam and the African-American community that would compare the size and characteristics of Islam within the black community in general; the relationship of that community to worldwide Islamic beliefs and practices, and with Islam among black inmates in jails and prisons. What can be said with certainty, however, is that the problem of racism mixed with religion exists within facilities, and must be dealt with by chaplains.

THE ATMOSPHERE AT RELIGIOUS SERVICES

The reason that the civil authorities put up with such interfaith hassling rests on a point of law. Those who are incarcerated cannot be denied the exercise of their religion. Essentially this means that congregating for religious services must be allowed for faith groups whose members are prisoners within the facility.

In describing chapel services as a social meeting time filled with whispered conversations, contraband passing, hand holding trysts and the barked commands of officers, Mark Benney observes that "nowhere do forms of worship take on more obviously empty, meaningless conventions" (1948:69). This is not always the case. When all goes well the chapel services of inmates can be as heartfelt and beautiful as any religious services experienced in the outside world. Nevertheless, the call for chapel provides an opportunity for inmates from different tier areas to congregate and meet for whatever purposes they choose, and this can create problems of both security and discipline (Note 13).

Father Patrick J. Ryan, writing in *America* in September 1992, recalls celebrating mass at the Riker's Island holding center and being advised by the French Little Sister of the Gospel who ministers there to eliminate the customary handshake at the sign of peace before communion. Her Gallic accent mangling American slang, she apologetically offered, "They sometimes use the opportunity to punch each other out" (1992:151). The only time I was physically hurt in all my time as a chaplain occurred during a brawl which erupted during mass when, while rolling on the floor with an inmate in an attempt to subdue him after he attacked another inmate, my hand was cut. Obviously things can get out hand in chapel.

When matters get really bad while working on the tiers and one's nerves seem about to snap the solution can be a simple retreat from the scene. Chapel services are another matter. Aside from the possibility of physical danger, there is the frustration which comes from wanting to provide a religious service which offers comfort and instruction. Yet, some inmates who want such instruction and comfort will say that they will not attend chapel because they cannot stand the general Sunday-go-meetin' atmosphere. If this is offensive to a genuinely religious inmate, it can be equally and more so for the chaplain who is, by role, present to create an atmosphere of prayer.

In describing the atmosphere of services in jail I have come to use the analogy that it is like being in charge of a large, sometimes unruly, high school study hall. In my parish I measure the success of a liturgy in terms of the atmosphere of prayer which has been created. In the jails success is often measured by being able to get from start to finish without any problems. One has to stop mid-sermon or mid-prayer to silence conversations or disruptive activities. Officers interrupt to call inmates out for visits. Sometimes officers, present to keep inmates from being disruptive, converse with one another in a way that is more disruptive than inmate behavior. In short, the times for services can be the most stressful times of the week. One feels tense in anticipation of all that could go wrong at each service, and during them, feels a lack of control of the situation.

While chaplains did not rate unruly behavior in chapel as being particularly distressful, the responses indicated that when disruptiveness does occur it is quite bothersome to some. One respondent admitted: "Sunday worship can be very stressful. Some inmates act as unruly teenagers. I am loath to holler at men. I therefore internalize my frustration in an attempt to be kind and not show any ill temper" (46). In contrast (and indicating why disruptiveness would be rated low) another chaplain put the matter in context of the amount of time actually spent in chapel, pointing out that "the least part of the job is the worship service. It may be important to the chaplain, but it takes only one hour or so of an otherwise full schedule, and many inmates who see chaplains regularly do not necessarily attend services" (25).

Since chapel services take up one hour of an otherwise full schedule, a self-portrait of chaplains should give attention to the way they describe themselves in their relationships with inmates and in the context of working throughout the entirety of a facility.

NOTES

1. On the Likert scale, the chaplains in the initial survey rated "Working in a hidden ministry isolated from fellow clergy" at a frequency mean of 2.9, while the mean reflecting the intensity with which they felt this was rated at a mean of only 2.4, with 80% of the chaplains rating isolation a low 1-3. In the Federal system replication the frequency mean was 2.8; the intensity mean 2.2. with 83.5% of the chaplains ranking it 1-3 in discomfort.

2. The item "Being subject to two chains of command civil as well as religious" was mentioned nine times by chaplains in the initial survey as being particularly distressing. Sixty percent rated these cross pressures 3-5 as to frequency (the mean being 3.1). Over 50% rated the problem 3-5 on the intensity scale (the mean being 2.6). The Federal chaplains rated the item a 2.9 frequency mean with 62.4% rating it a 3-5 on the Likert scale; the intensity mean was 2.6, with 49.1% of the chaplains rating it a 3-5 on the intensity scale.

3. In the initial survey 71.4% of the chaplains rated "bureaucratic paper work required by the facility," 3-5 in frequency on the Likert scale (with a mean of 3.3) and 65.7% rated it 3-5 in intensity (with a mean of 3.0). One third of the chaplains (30%) rated paperwork a 5 (constant) in frequency of encounter. The Federal chaplains, who ranked this item highest as a stress factor, did so with a frequency mean of 4.1 and an intensity of distress mean of 3.8; 43.6% ranked paperwork a 5 in frequency of encounter.

4. The responses to the survey statement "Preaching about a loving God within a punishment setting" indicated that the chaplains clearly differentiated between the experienced frequency of a demand and its intensity. The problem was rated high in frequency (with a mean of 3.2) yet low in intensity as a distress factor (a mean of 2.1). The issue was rated as a 5 (i.e., as a factor often to be dealt with) by 35.7% of the chaplains. Yet, only 5.7% rated it as being significantly distressing. That disparity remained in the Federal replication; the mean for frequency was 3.0 while the mean for intensity of distress a 2.0.

5. The overall Likert scale response to the item "Conflict with Corrections Officers and other facility staff members" was moderate in the initial survey, with a dissenting minority who felt more strongly.: 62% of chaplains rated the item a 2-3 as to the frequency of concern, and 22.9% rated it a 4-5 in frequency (the mean being 2.7); 54% rated it a 2-3 in intensity of distress, and nearly a third of the chaplains (32.9%) rated it a high 4-5 in intensity (with 2.8 as the mean). In the Federal replication, 78.7% rated it a 2-3 in frequency while a lesser number, 13% rated it 4-5 (with a mean of 2.7). Even without the slight polarization, the mean of distress was 3.0.

6. The problem of "Living in a prison reality where mores are dictated by inmate codes," was recognized by the chaplains (the mean score for experienced frequency equaled 3.1). On the other hand, the chaplains were not distressed by this problem. Half of them used 1 or 2 on the scale measuring intensity of concern, and the mean distress score for the sample was only 2.7. In the Federal level replication the mean for frequency was slightly lower, 2.8, as was the mean for distress, 2.5.

7. The chaplains did not rate the issue "having to balance nonjudgmental sympathy with the preaching of morality" as being a significant problem, the mean for frequency being 2.8 (2.6 in the Federal) and for intensity, 2.2. (2.3 in the Federal).

8. The item *reacting emotionally against the dislikable personalities of some inmates* did not strike the chaplains as very serious. The mean for both frequency and intensity was 2.7, both in the State level and Federal level surveys.

9. Eighty five percent of the initial respondents rated the item, "Dealing with simplistic attitudes about offenders," 3-5 in frequency; 48.6% rating it 4-5 (the mean was 3.5). Sixty eight percent rated the concern as 3-5 in intensity of distress; 30% rating it 4-5 (the mean was 3.1). The Federal chaplains rated this lower, the frequency mean being 3.0 and the intensity mean, 2.6. The disparity might well reflect the distance of Federal inmates from their own home areas, and the corresponding fact that these chaplains, even if they are serving an outside congregation, are dealing with congregations far removed in distance from the crimes committed by the inmates involved.

10. In the Likert scale response chaplains in the initial survey rated frictions with fellow chaplains a frequency mean of 2.4 and intensity mean of 2.6; the Federal chaplains rated it a similar 2.5 in frequency and 2.8 in intensity.

11. Chaplains rated the item "Dealing with volunteer groups" a mean of 2.7 on the Likert scale for frequency, and a mean of 2.5 for intensity. Federal chaplains scored this a slightly higher 2.8 in frequency and a 3.0 in intensity of distress.

12. Over two thirds of the chaplains in the initial survey rated the item "racial religious tensions" a 3-5 in experienced frequency (mean 3.0) and 67.1% rated it

a 3-5 on the intensity of distress it produces (mean 2.9). The Federal chaplains rated it similarly, with a frequency mean of 3.0 and an intensity mean of 2.9.

13. Seventy percent of the chaplains in the first survey rated "Unruly behavior at religious services" 1-2 in frequency of encounter (with a mean of 2.1) and 61.4% rated it a 1-2 in intensity of concern (with a mean of 2.3). The Federal chaplains followed suit, rating the item a low 1.8 mean in frequency and a correspondingly low 2.0 in intensity of distress.

► **Table 4-1: Distribution of Likert Scale Responses among New York State Chaplains**

- **Items Relating to Institution**   **PROBLEM FREQUENCY**

	0	1	2	3	4	5	Mean
1: Noise factor	0	4	25	17	15	9	3.00
2: Physical danger	0	18	27	12	9	4	2.34
3: Contracting illness	0	23	25	10	8	4	2.21
4: Invasion of privacy	2	14	18	21	9	6	2.56
5: Dealing with opposite sex	24	26	5	4	6	5	1.39
6: Love v. punishment	1	15	11	8	10	25	3.23
7: Overcrowding	0	8	8	12	20	22	3.57
8: Unruly services	0	24	25	14	3	4	2.11
9: Two chains of command	0	9	19	12	13	17	3.14
10: Paperwork	2	8	10	16	13	21	3.33
11: Injustice	0	1	6	20	28	15	3.70
12: Ministry inside/outside	4	21	14	12	7	12	2.47
13: Public attitudes	0	2	9	25	19	15	3.51
14: Isolation from clergy	0	14	19	10	14	13	2.90

STRESS INTENSITY

	0	1	2	3	4	5	Mean
1: Noise factor	0	11	21	25	7	6	2.66
2: Physical danger	0	31	22	13	2	2	1.89
3: Contracting illness	0	33	19	12	3	3	1.91
4: Invasion of privacy	3	23	19	17	7	1	2.07
5: Dealing with opposite sex	26	27	4	7	4	2	1.17
6: Love v. punishment	1	31	16	9	9	4	2.09
7: Overcrowding	1	8	9	17	21	14	3.30
8: Unruly services	0	22	21	12	9	6	2.37
9: Two chains of command	0	18	15	18	11	8	2.66
10: Paperwork	2	10	12	17	19	10	3.01
11: Injustice	0	1	8	23	22	16	3.61
12: Ministry inside/outside	4	27	15	11	8	5	2.10
13: Public attitudes	0	3	19	27	12	9	3.07
14: Isolation from clergy	0	22	14	20	7	7	2.47

▶ **Table 4-1 [Continued]**

● **Items Relating to Inmates**   **PROBLEM FREQUENCY**

	0	1	2	3	4	5	Mean
15: Social chasm	0	9	30	17	11	3	2.56
16: Being conned	0	3	29	26	5	7	2.77
17: Recidivism	1	2	17	24	17	9	3.16
18: Same old stories	1	5	13	14	25	12	3.33
19: Family crises	1	2	10	29	17	11	3.31
20: Emotional involvement	2	7	25	22	10	4	2.61
21: Morals v. nonjudgmentalism	3	6	22	14	19	6	2.83
22: Personalities	2	1	33	21	9	4	2.66
23: Mentally ill	2	5	27	13	16	7	2.81
24: Confidences	1	10	34	18	5	2	2.31
25: Inmate mores	2	5	17	14	19	13	3.17
26: Racial/religious conflict	1	5	16	23	18	7	3.04
27: Conflict with volunteers	1	9	22	20	15	3	2.69
28: Friction: Corrections Officers, staff	1	6	27	20	10	6	2.71
29: Interdenominational friction	1	13	31	14	6	5	2.37

STRESS INTENSITY

	0	1	2	3	4	5	Mean
15: Social chasm	0	16	29	17	6	2	2.27
16: Being conned	0	10	12	26	13	9	2.99
17: Recidivism	1	7	15	26	13	8	2.96
18: Same old stories	1	13	25	16	11	4	2.50
19: Family crises	1	6	14	25	15	9	3.06
20: Emotional involvement	1	7	27	22	11	2	2.59
21: Morals v. nonjudgmentalism	3	18	25	13	8	3	2.20
22: Personalities	2	5	23	25	10	5	2.73
23: Mentally ill	2	8	20	13	15	12	2.96
24: Confidences	1	14	29	15	9	2	2.33
25: Inmate mores	2	11	22	13	15	7	2.70
26: Racial/religious conflict	1	7	15	25	16	6	2.94
27: Conflict with volunteers	1	15	22	16	10	6	2.53
28: Friction: Corrections Officers, staff	1	8	25	13	16	7	2.80
29: Interdenominational friction	1	16	21	15	9	8	2.56

► **Table 4-2: Distribution of Likert Scale Responses among Federal System Chaplains**

• **Items Relating to Institution**   **PROBLEM FREQUENCY**

	0	1	2	3	4	5	Mean
1: Noise factor	1	10	33	49	16	4	2.74
2: Physical danger	1	27	51	19	10	5	2.23
3: Contracting illness	2	32	50	15	8	6	2.15
4: Invasion of privacy	7	27	29	33	13	4	2.42
5: Dealing with opposite sex	21	62	13	9	5	3	1.63
6: Love v. punishment	5	29	13	17	20	29	3.07
7: Overcrowding	3	10	13	13	37	37	3.71
8: Unruly services	5	44	50	8	3	3	1.81
9: Two chains of command	4	16	25	38	16	14	2.88
10: Paperwork	3	2	7	13	40	48	4.14
11: Injustice	6	4	20	35	36	12	3.30
12: Ministry inside/outside	11	52	21	18	9	2	1.90
13: Public attitudes	4	7	26	37	31	8	3.06
14: Isolation from clergy	4	22	29	22	24	12	2.77

STRESS INTENSITY

	0	1	2	3	4	5	Mean
1: Noise factor	2	24	30	38	15	4	2.51
2: Physical danger	2	48	36	19	4	4	1.92
3: Contracting illness	2	51	36	9	9	6	1.95
4: Invasion of privacy	8	39	27	26	8	5	2.17
5: Dealing with opposite sex	19	63	9	11	7	4	1.72
6: Love v. punishment	5	49	24	20	11	4	2.05
7: Overcrowding	3	12	15	23	32	28	3.45
8: Unruly services	5	43	34	16	10	5	2.07
9: Two chains of command	5	23	32	27	18	8	2.59
10: Paperwork	4	3	13	24	36	33	3.76
11: Injustice	7	6	21	28	35	16	3.32
12: Ministry inside/outside	11	63	16	16	6	1	1.69
13: Public attitudes	3	20	29	40	15	6	2.62
14: Isolation from clergy	4	32	35	24	16	2	2.28

► *Table 4-2 [Continued]*

• *Items Relating to Inmates*			*PROBLEM FREQUENCY*				
	0	1	2	3	4	5	Mean
15: Social chasm	4	12	31	42	21	3	2.74
16: Being conned	4	4	46	49	10	0	2.50
17: Recidivism	8	11	34	36	22	2	2.71
18: Same old stories	4	9	25	40	34	1	2.94
19: Family crises	6	7	20	39	32	9	3.15
20: Emotional involvement	9	11	42	38	12	1	2.52
21: Morals v. nonjudgmentalism	10	18	27	32	22	4	2.68
22: Personalities	7	8	37	45	14	2	2.67
23: Mentally ill	5	14	44	32	14	4	2.54
24: Confidences	8	22	44	32	5	2	2.25
25: Inmate mores	12	8	36	29	22	6	2.82
26: Racial/religious conflict	9	35	30	23	10	9	2.96
27: Conflict with volunteers	7	7	40	33	20	6	2.79
28: Friction: Corrections Officers, staff	5	9	36	49	12	2	2.65
29: Interdenominational friction	4	18	40	36	10	5	2.49

			STRESS INTENSITY				
	0	1	2	3	4	5	Mean
15: Social chasm	5	25	30	35	12	6	2.48
16: Being conned	7	24	33	34	10	5	3.15
17: Recidivism	8	18	33	33	19	2	2.56
18: Same old stories	4	21	34	36	16	2	2.49
19: Family crises	10	6	23	28	37	9	3.19
20: Emotional involvement	11	17	32	38	11	4	2.52
21: Morals v. nonjudgmentalism	11	28	29	36	9	0	2.26
22: Personalities	8	12	39	29	22	3	2.67
23: Mentally ill	5	19	25	35	23	6	2.74
24: Confidences	10	35	29	20	12	7	2.29
25: Inmate mores	13	15	40	25	16	4	2.54
26: Racial/religious conflict	9	13	24	35	25	7	2.89
27: Conflict with volunteers	5	8	29	30	31	10	3.06
28: Friction: Corrections Officers, staff	5	12	27	31	21	17	3.04
29: Interdenominational friction	4	20	28	25	11	4	2.81

► **Table 4-3: Mean Ranking of Likert Scale Items in Relative Rank Order among New York State Chaplains**

FREQUENCY OF OCCURRENCE		INTENSITY OF DEMAND	
1: Injustice	3.70	1: Injustice	3.61
2: Overcrowding	3.57	2: Overcrowding	3.30
3: Public Attitudes	3.51	3: Public Attitudes	3.07
4: Paperwork	3.33	4: Family Crises	3.06
5: Same Old Stories	3.33	5: Paperwork	3.01
6: Family Crises	3.31	6: Being conned	2.99
7: Love v. Punish	3.23	7: Recidivism	2.96
8: Inmate mores	3.17	8: Mentally Ill	2.96
9: Recidivism	3.16	9: Race/Religion	2.94
10: Two Authorities	3.14	10: Corrections Officers and Staff	2.80
11: Race/Religion	3.04	11: Personalities	2.73
12: Noise	3.00	12: Inmate mores	2.70
13: Isolation	2.90	13: Two Authorities	2.66
14: Morals v. nonjudgmentalism	2.83	14: Noise	2.66
15: Mentally ill	2.81	15: Emotional involvement	2.59
16: Being conned	2.77	16: Denominational Friction	2.56
17: Corrections Officers and Staff	2.71	17: Volunteers	2.53
18: Volunteers	2.69	18: Same Old Stories	2.50
19: Personalities	2.66	19: Isolation	2.47
20: Emotional involvement	2.61	20: Unruly services	2.37
21: Social chasm	2.56	21: Confidences	2.33
22: Invasion of Privacy	2.56	22: Social chasm	2.27
23: Ministry In/out	2.47	23: Morals v. nonjudgmentalism	2.22
24: Denominational friction	2.37	24: Ministry In/out	2.10
25: Physical Danger	2.34	25: Love v. Punish	2.09
26: Confidences	2.31	26: Invasion of Privacy	2.07
27: Illness	2.21	27: Illness	1.91
28: Unruly services	2.11		

► **Table 4.4: Mean Ranking of Likert Scale Items in Relative Rank Order among Federal Chaplains**

FREQUENCY OF OCCURRENCE		INTENSITY OF DEMAND	
1: Paperwork	4.14	1: Paperwork	3.76
2: Overcrowding	3.71	2: Overcrowding	3.45
3: Injustice	3.30	3: Injustice	3.32
4: Family Crises	3.15	4: Family Crises	3.19
5: Love v. Punish	3.07	5: Being conned	3.15
6: Public Attitudes	3.06	6: Volunteers	3.06
7: Race/Religion	2.96	7: Corrections Officers and Staff	3.04
8: Same Old Stories	2.94	8: Race/Religion	2.89
9: Two Authorities	2.88	9: Denominational Friction	2.81
10: Inmate Mores	2.82	10: Mentally Ill	2.74
11: Volunteers	2.79	11: Personalities	2.67
12: Isolation	2.77	12: Public Attitudes	2.62
13: Noise	2.74	13: Two Authorities	2.59
14: Social Chasm	2.74	14: Recidivism	2.56
15: Recidivism	2.71	15: Inmate Mores	2.54
16: Morals v. Nonjudgementalism	2.68	16: Emotional Involvement	2.54
17: Personalities	2.67	17: Noise	2.51
18: Corrections Officers and Staff	2.65	18: Same Old stories	2.49
19: Being Conned	2.60	19: Social Chasm	2.48
20: Mentally Ill	2.54	20: Confidences	2.29
21: Emotional Involvement	2.52	21: Isolated	2.28
22: Denominational Friction	2.49	22: Morals v. Nonjudgementalism	2.26
23: Invasion of Privacy	2.42	23: Invasion of Privacy	2.17
24: Confidences	2.25	24: Unruly Services	2.07
25: Danger	2.23	25: Love v. Punish	2.05
26: Illness	2.15	26: Illness	1.95
27: Ministry In/Out	1.90	27: Danger	1.92
28: Unruly Services	1.81	28: Opposite Sex	1.72
29: Opposite Sex	1.63	29: Ministry In/Out	1.69

Chapter 5

SHARING LIFE WITH THE INCARCERATED

Prison and jail facilities are almost always immediately identifiable to passersby because of their exteriors of concrete and steel, surrounded by barbed wire fencing. Whatever else may be attempted or accomplished within penal institutions, security is the prime concern of those who run them, and rightly so, since most of these hold a great many individuals who have been judged dangerous because of their behavior on the streets. Moreover, as is evidenced in this nation's history of prison disturbances, some prisoners are capable of using extreme violence to gain objectives, either as individuals or in groups.

In accepting a ministry in jail/prison chaplaincy, one is accepting a daily task of intermingling with potentially dangerous individuals on tiers, in yards, in hallways, recreation areas, mess halls, and above all during crowded chapel services — which, in many facilities is the largest gathering of inmates from tier areas who would otherwise have had no contact with each other. If an inmate action of some sort is planned, chapel service provides a perfect time and place to target such an action, as exemplified in *Papillon*, in which an escape plan centers on taking a priest hostage during mass.

In 1985, the Rev. George Brucker, leaving the Schenectady County Jail after services, was grabbed and used as a shield by a weapon-wielding inmate in midst of a successful escape. Shortly after this, in the Rensselaer County Jail, where I serve as chaplain, an inmate named Roy began showing a sudden interest in religion not long after his conviction for murder. Each Sunday, following services, in the general confusion which always accompanies the return of inmates to the tier areas, Roy made a habit of coming up to the altar and engaging me in a theological inquiry. I had hitherto enjoyed Roy as a conversationalist. He is an intelligent and witty person. However, he had also killed a man during a robbery and had vowed a number of times on the tiers that he was not going to stay in prison for 25 years to life.

For a month or so, Roy kept going through the uncharacteristic, religious questions game while COs and inmates headed for the hallway area. I finally mentioned to an officer that I wanted him to "notice" the theology discussions in the coming weeks and to make it obvious that the conversations were being observed. With this, the game ceased. Roy's ambitions of escaping did not. He eventually sawed his way through bars near his tier end shower area, squeezed through and jumped to a nearbye garage roof. He enjoyed liberty for a few days during which the media, for their part, enjoyed a festival of colorful coverage — of which I was happy not to have been a part.

It was while Roy was voicing his intentions of escaping that, on his tier one day, I happened to look upward and noticed the barely visible point of something protruding over the ledge of the bars. "Hello, what's this?" I asked, reaching up to take a razor in my hands. The response, understandably, was dead silence; no one was about to claim it. Nor was I about to give it to the group and say, "See that the rightful owner gets it."

Thoughts of Rev. George Brucker, and of this razor being held to my throat, were not idle fancy. Later, I placed the razor on a sergeant's desk, and, when asked, refused to say where I had found it. I wanted security staff to know that one of them was not doing his job thoroughly. I was not, however, going to compromise my role and do that job for them.

Occasionally a particular inmate will cause wariness — even fear — within, at least, this chaplain. Charlie Thomas was a muscular, Vietnam veteran, on disability for having lost part of a foot. Heavily into weight lifting — and young boys as sex objects — Charlie was a rich man by jail standards owing to his regular disability check. Youngsters, rewarded with money in commissary accounts, fought to sit thigh-to-thigh next to Charlie in chapel.

Charlie also had more free money than many officers. I would constantly see him in places where he had no business to be, often on the catwalks of the "kiddie tier." Wary of Charlie, who was equally wary of me, I would always see that a wall was to my back if I was on a tier and Charlie slipped on to it. I did not want Charlie behind me. Charlie eventually raped a boy in a shower area of the kiddie tier, and the boy's family pressed charges not only against Charlie but against the jail and the officer who was bribed to allow Charlie into the shower area. In this case, the Officer was convicted and went to prison along with Charlie — as his fellow prisoner. The added frustration for a chaplain in a situation such as this is in not being able to cross roles, to play the officer and blow the whistle in advance on people like Charlie. But to wish for this is to wish for omniscience and omnipresence.

One danger factor which affects jail chaplains more than prison chaplains is that they must deal with local inmates on the streets as well as in the jail. This would include inmates who have decided that the chaplain is, for whatever reason, an enemy. One college age inmate, ironically the son of a respected clergyman in the Albany area, had gone the Satanic Cult, heavy drug, metal rock route and had fried his brain with a number of substances for several years. Wild-eyed and visionary, he spent a number of months on our mental tier, never quite drying into reality. Locked into a Satanic, mirror view of religion, he would tell me, apologetically and sincerely, that he was supposed to kill me.

Shortly after his release, I was at a high school cross-country meet in Albany's Washington Park. Moments before the race was to begin, my Satanic acquaintance, looking more gaunt than ever, appeared in front of me and began his usual overture of assassination. However, this time there were no bars between us and he insisted that he had a gun in his coat pocket. Later, when I could relate the incident in a perspective of humor I told others that I imagined him shooting me; the runners mistaking the sound for the starting gun, and my death being so ignoble as to mean nothing more than the false start of a race. The humor came later. At the moment the incident created no little fear within me.

Although 91.4% of the chaplains of New York State who responded to the survey minister in medium and maximum security facilities, only 5.7% listed danger as a constant problem and in the Federal system this dropped to 4.5%. None of the chaplains expanded upon danger as a stress factor. One priest serving at a medium security facility commented: "Much of what you see, especially in movies and television is false and is mere sensationalism. Prison life is very monotonous" (25).

And it is. Conditioning sets in and even that which might be categorized as dangerous becomes routine. When this writer/chaplain entered this ministry in the early 1970s I initially felt a pervasive sense of fear, owing to my surroundings. This gradually dissipated. After several years one simply does not think of danger even if it does exist. Earlier in the same week in which I write this, I was standing in the main hallway of Albany County Jail when the alarms sounded, indicating an emergency which could have been almost anything; a fight, a fire, an officer accosted by an inmate, etc. Inmates coming from recreation were in the hall. As officers ran through the hallway to the area where they were called I backed against the wall with the inmates present. One of them, in derision, chanted: "hup-two three-four hup-two-three-four," and I didn't think anything of the taunt, or much of the emergency situation. Neither did those officers seasoned by time on the job. It was just part of the day. Harm may have come from what was occurring, but there was little use in worrying about it. It is a matter of conditioning (Note 1).

THE DANGER OF CONTRACTING ILLNESS

As the spread of AIDS became a problem in society in the 1980s, it became a severe problem in facilities which house growing numbers of those afflicted, as well as the greatest at risk population with regards to contracting the illness. This caught everyone in corrections off guard and at first no one knew quite what to do or how to react in practical terms. A priest working in a medium security state prison reacted to this, stating that "the ostracization of HIV positive inmates within the system and among their peers is, in my opinion, the single most stressful factor that this ministry places upon chaplains today" (23). In 1985 the first diagnosed case of AIDS that appeared in the Albany County Jail reflected the fear which accompanied it. In an incident reported sensationally in the media, a newly released prison parolee who had full blown AIDS raped an Albany woman, bit her, and told her that she now had AIDS as well. Incarcerated, the man constantly threatened to bite officers. In a photo printed in the Albany *Times Union*, he was shown being brought to court with his hands cuffed behind his back, a surgical mask tied around his face.

At the jail, the man was locked in a room on the nurse's tier. When COs had to go in to him they wore protective clothing for fear of his teeth, which, under the circumstances, were far more dangerous than any knife. For three days I put off going to see this inmate. Finally, my conscience persuaded me that this was part of my job. This man's case was the first, but more would follow, and I had to begin sometime. I refused to put on protective clothing; that seemed a denial of role. I went into his room, sat on his bed, and we talked for a long time. A few days later the inmate told me that he wished to receive Holy Communion.

Again I wrestled within myself. Should I tell him that he had to take the host in his hand rather than have the option of me placing it on his tongue? Was his meekness with me thus far a ruse so that he could sink his teeth into my fingers at a moment which he would find most ironical? I must admit that I was genuinely terrified, although nothing did happen to justify my fears.

In 1987 a special tier was set aside in my institution for AIDS diagnosed inmates. At first, officers assigned to work the tier complained about the assignment. Gradually, as with other dangers, AIDS became accepted as a reality of jail life. So, too, the great majority of chaplains who responded to the survey quickly learned to deal with the illness (Note 2). A priest ministering in a maximum security facility which houses many lifers commented that in his first ten years at the place he had two inmate funerals. Within the preceding two years, he had buried a dozen men, all of whom had died of AIDS related complications. An Imam, likewise serving in a maximum security facility, suggested: "There should be separate facilities for inmates with AIDS or hepatitis. The constant thought of the possibility of contracting this disease is sometimes distressing" (47).

As of this writing AIDS, still without a cure, continues to spread. Everyone remains uncomfortable with it. Officers must sometimes subdue inmates, and chaplains must accept that distraught inmates cling to them, and in times of stress, slobber on them. No less frightening is the occasional contact with an inmate who has been cut and is bleeding. Recently I encountered an angry young inmate rushing out into our main hallway from the visiting area where he had had a violent argument with his girlfriend. Still angry, he took out his frustrations by yelling at me. Suddenly and irrationally, he swung at me. As I recoiled he lost his balance and put his fist through window behind me, smashing the glass and tearing through the inner mesh wiring.

The sight of his own gushing blood reduced him to staring at his hand in something like shock. Women carrying babies were leaving the visiting area. If the alarms went off and officers rushed the scene a needless panic could have been created. Hoping to avert this I grabbed the inmate's wrist, his flowing blood running over my hand as well as his, held him up by putting my arm around his shoulder, and quietly beckoned an officer for assistance. Later in the nurse's office, washing his blood from my right hand I began examining my fingers, nervously pondering, "In this day and age a papercut could make me history."

HUMAN WAREHOUSING

The overcrowding which results from warehousing, described by a chaplain at a State facility for women as "the constant flow of people into the system or returning to the system" (19) hits home as an issue to chaplains (Note 3).

"One hundred percent overcrowding is the biggest [stress] factor," decided a minister at a medium security Federal prison (39). Another minister, serving at a minimum security State facility, noted that the level of overcrowding in his facility was "symbolized by the conversion of the gym into a dormitory with no gym to use for perhaps the past 1.5 years" (20).

Such overcrowding often results in a breakdown of classifications which are meant to keep different categories of inmates separate (e.g., minors from adults; violent criminals from lesser offenders). While administrators can assure the public that such categories are being adhered to as required by law, what they mean is that a technicality is bowed to while a reality is ignored. For instance, minors are housed on tiers with adults but are considered as being separated because the two groups are kept locked in their cells at separate times. Total contact remains for purposes of threatening, spitting, touching, whatever.

The overcrowded warehousing of humans acerbates the injustice of the bottom-of-the-pile treatment of women within a system where they need not equal but special care. A woman minister wrote: "With the increase in female institutions there are different needs, more counseling need for women in following: Counseling women who are losing their children to adoption, lack of family support (females are more committed to standing by the men than males are to standing by the woman), and re-entry to society seems to be easier for men — social stigmatizing for women is more devastating" (2).

In county jails throughout the United States, where inmates are generally housed in the same building as male inmates, women's tiers seem to be added as if they were an afterthought. They are crammed in inaccessible areas of a facility, and, because men and women are kept strictly segregated, women are denied equal opportunities to work as trustees in the kitchen, around the grounds, in the library, and in offices. They are often deprived of the use of the facility's gym, or made to use it at an odd hour.

Women are often more callously treated than men if one holds to an opinion that women are more sensitive to matters of personal privacy. In a brusque, male dominated realm they are subject to dehumanizing, yelled commands such as: "Feed the females," and "Run the females for church." The latter command is hardly a conducive invitation to inspire in anyone a desire to attend a service of worship.

Chaplaincy is largely a male occupation and this can lead to a stressful sense of failure in a ministry to the incarcerated. A man cannot help but feel that he is invading the privacy of others when entering a women's housing area. A woman corrections officer must remain nearby, to protect not only the privacy of the women but to ensure the reputation of the clergyman. Hamstrung by this, a chaplain can be limited in his abilities to understand and feel just what women are suffering in an incarcerated situation.

Joan Potter's article "In Prison, Women are Different" is illustrated with a photo of a black chaplain attempting to talk to a mentally disturbed inmate. She is lying on the cot in her cell with a sheet pulled over her head. Outsided the cell he leans against the bars, and seems to be having no effect in speaking with her. His slumped body posture is evidence of frustration in failure (1978:34). Were it not for the help of women volunteer groups, male chaplains would be even more hamstrung in ministering to incarcerated women (Note 4).

INJUSTICES WITHIN THE SYSTEM

Societal biases built into the penal system prompted the chaplains to decry "the systemized treating of men and women as children with no responsibility for their own lives," (68) and the "terrible bias toward locking up the poor, black and Hispanic" (36). Disparity in sentencing, a constant topic of inmate conversation on tiers, is a reality which not only causes distress for them, but for chaplains as well who can only listen and feel frustrations along with the imprisoned (Note 5).

"The new Federal law mandating mandatory two thirds sentence; the abolition of parole and the reinstatement of capital punishment are moral abuses causing me stress," (42) shared one chaplain. Another personalized the matter, bringing it to a tier level where prisoners seek to recruit chaplains to serve "as advocates in borderline cases wherein principles of justice are clear but their application in a particular instance is relatively questionable" (23). Oftentimes one wakes up in the middle of the night wondering about the alleged guilt of a particular inmate, wondering if an innocent victim of society's misjudgment is being railroaded.

For example, as this is written, a woman inmate has just left our jail for state prison. She was convicted of having her husband killed by a hit man she hired. Throughout the many months of her incarceration in our facility, she firmly and calmly maintained that she is innocent. She is pleasant, warm-hearted, and generous with other inmates. She tutors in the jail school and is that rarity among inmates, someone with a strong church background who knows, appreciates, and helps to put together a good liturgy in chapel. I do not want to believe, as a jury believed, that she is guilty of cold-blooded murder. Not being Solomon, much less God, a chaplain can be anguished by such wonderings.

Other injustices within facilities result from a bureaucratic view of keeping the letter of the law. As noted by one chaplain: "In prison, what is written on one's rap sheet can cause undue harm and grief to prisoners. In my facility even the suggestion, not proof of a sex crime deprives one of outside clearance, family reunion program furlough, and work release. Charges are not erased from rap sheets unless the lawyer, after the court decision, insists such charges be noted as untrue or unproven" (35).

Just as socio-economic background and political power affect court practices, so too they cause differential treatment behind bars. Preference can be accorded those prisoners who have power in the outside world. A jailed politician can be housed on a nurse's tier in a comfortable room (with an air conditioner in one memorable Albany County Jail instance). Rules can be stretched according to inmate pull.

On one occasion this chaplain ended up in an eyeball-to-eyeball standoff with two deputies at a funeral home in Albany's inner city. The officers insisted on returning a black inmate to jail before the funeral service when the inmate's family arrived 40 minutes late. They insisted that their orders allowed an hour out of the jail and refused to be flexible about the matter. Only a phone appeal to the sheriff and a grudging allowance on his part permitted the delay. When the family finally appeared, hurried prayers were said. It was the sort of everyday chaplaincy tug of war which causes ulcers.

Juxtaposed with this incident, later that same day at the jail, I witnessed a new inmate being allowed a contact visit with his family outside of visiting hours. In addition to this rule, a second rule was also being waived, one which forbids any contact visit during the first seven days of an inmate's incarceration. This new inmate, however, had a great deal more outside influence than the black, poor inmate for whose right to remain at a family funeral I had to fight earlier in the day. The new arrival was a wealthy businessman, being given a slap on the wrist, via a month-long sentence for income tax evasion involving thousands of dollars. The concept of "rules" meant something different in the two separate cases.

As embittering as this sort of situation is to a chaplain who becomes caught in the middle of such slide rule justice, he must remember that he is equally called to minister to each of the differently treated inmates. If the black and poor inmate needed comfort, so too did this wealthy man whose wife and children sat with him, in tears, experiencing for the first time a world which for them had existed only in entertainment media. Still, such disparity causes a great deal of frustration to any fair-minded chaplain.

THE MENTALLY ILL, ADDICTED, AND HOMELESS

County jails tend to be dumping grounds for people who slip through the cracks of the system. These include the homeless and mentally ill who often exist on a sad unmerry-go-round of outpatient psychiatric clinics, the streets, and jail. They are rarely charged with anything serious — usually shoplifting or criminal trespass (e.g., sleeping on a heating grate of City Hall) — and they sit for months in jail because no one knows what to do with them. Neither do chaplains who indicated that this problem bothers them considerably by rating it higher in the distress it causes than in its frequency of occurrence (Note 6). "It is very difficult to know where you are with mental inmates," observed a chaplain (12), to which another added, they "cannot obtain proper care in a prison setting" (23). Reflecting commonly felt helplessness a priest at a large metropolitan jail said: "With mentally ill patients I contact the clinic for advice — or else I just listen and pray" (55).

Injustice goes beyond legalities when the system fails to provide needed help for offenders regardless of their guilt or innocence. One chaplain decried the "lack of programs addressing the drug issue" (19) and another broadened this complaint to include "poor therapy programs for all" (3).

"The big complaint that I have," said a third, "is the lack of places to accept men after their incarceration. So many more could be saved from returning if halfway houses were available" (1). For some chaplains society's failures were internalized. "I am always aware (painfully) that there is very little support for these people when they have been released," wrote one, "I try to keep up some contacts — letters — phone calls — but I find I cannot care for them at all sufficiently when they are out — or even when they are in. Inadequacy" (66).

DEALING WITH TRAGEDIES AND FAMILY CRISES

If, at this writing, AIDS means an inexorable, slow death, abrupt death all too frequently occurs in jail with suicides. When a suicide does occur in a facility there is a great sense of frustration and a sense of having failed in one's job on the part of many staff members, officers, social workers, and, of course, chaplains. One wonders if the inmate had, with some word or gesture, issued a warning or a cry for help which was not noticed or not taken seriously. In the early 1980s a girl of 16 girl hanged herself in Albany County Jail several days before Christmas. She did it shortly after I had gone about distributing greeting cards for the inmates to send out. I was very busy with "busy" work. Later I tortured myself wondering if she had tried to tell me something when I had handed her packet of cards to her.

The great majority of inmates doing time in prison are separated in distance from their families. When tragedies occur, and the chaplain is called upon to console the grieving inmate, he or she is limited to having to share in the enforced separation. There is seldom the opportunity to sit with a family drawn together by grief as would be possible if dealing in a neighborhood congregation or parish setting. Ministering to an inmate in such a situation would have to involve frustration for both parties.

When it is logistically possible most facilities will transport an inmate to either the wake or the funeral of an immediate family member. The inmates are brought handcuffed. Whether they remain handcuffed during the service depends on the seriousness of the inmate's criminal record, the situation, and which officers do the transporting. Obviously, a high risk offender is still considered a risk even at such a time. A nonviolent property offender, or a teenager whose mother has died, presents a case open to the discretion of the accompanying officers. I have watched officers reach over and quietly uncuff an inmate once they are inside the church or funeral parlor. I have also, with embarrassment for my position as a member of the jail's personnel, been part of situations where a sobbing youngster is kept cuffed because the officer present refuses to accept that there is no way on earth the child would bolt his mother's funeral. One cannot press the matter much beyond a suggestion because such an officer is acting within the dictates of the rule. A middle-aged black woman, brought to her brother's funeral, beckoned to me and whispered a request: Could she borrow my handkerchief? She did not use it to wipe away the tears that were streaming down her face but to cover the cuffs as she sat with her hands on her lap.

To be a party to all this and be unable to change can be deeply stressful. "Dealing with inmates' family crises when it is beyond your means to alleviate the situation (e.g., by obtaining a furlough, etc.)," drew a fairly strong response from the chaplains (Note 7). One chaplain, already quoted in another context, pointed out that it was difficult to build a sense of community within a prison setting because of the background of fractured family lives of the inmates: " . . . family life does not exist for inmates, or, if it does, it is so badly disrupted that family life will be a pain rather than joy" (26). Another pointed to the need of working with the inmates' families when it is possible: "Visiting room and work areas should be visited, and ministry to families is on the rise. A meeting of the family together with the inmate clarifies many situations" (5).

The other side of the issue of sorting out family crises is that prison and jail personnel deal with street smart people some of whom are willing to use even the idea of tragedy to gain an immediate advantage. Just as a facility's medical staff becomes jaded at hearing endless woes about pain and illnesses which, if believed, will gain an inmate mind-softening medication, so too, jail switchboards are often overloaded with non-documented "emergency" phone calls. An occasional voice over a phone insists that a particular inmate must be spoken to because of a family tragedy which ultimately turns out to be nonexistent. The chaplain frequently gets caught in the middle of this game and must operate without a psychic talent to discern real emergencies from bogus ploys.

In prisons, a chaplain's office phone becomes a target for inmates who can convince him that they need calls beyond those which the facility allows them. In the local county jail world, so near to most inmates' homes, the chaplain naturally becomes involved in many family situations, both important and trivial. I have come to refer to the list of phone messages which I take from the tiers each day as my "grocery list." The messages include pleadings to relatives and friends for visits, clothes, commissary money, etc. One becomes a vital link for some families. One man, in state prison now, requests that I visit his mother every now and then in a local nursing home. She suffers from Alzheimer's disease and doesn't know who I am, but it consoles him that I can write to him of some small detail, such as the color of her robe, etc.

Nevertheless, one makes rules for oneself after hard experiences. One rule which this chaplain has learned to follow is to never get involved as an intermediary in a case which is still pending between spouses or lovers, when a domestic dispute has put one in jail by the accusations of the other. A chaplain can be conned into being an extension of a harassing individual and becomes, himself, the harassing party.

If battling couples are a problem, lovers who want to marry are not always far behind them. In county jails, spouses who are both incarcerated in the same facility can visit one another. There are some inmates who would marry an acquaintance on the other side of the jail just to get a contact visit with someone of the opposite sex. A chaplain is constantly besieged with the request — "Can I get married while I'm in here?" Even when agreeing to an inmate's right to marry a chaplain often finds himself talking to a brick wall, attempting to make an inmate see the difference between a civil and a religious marriage; between a justice of the peace and a minister of religion. Often, prisoners could care less. They simply want to tie the knot. It is a matter of no little complexity to have to be consistent in applying behind prison walls the same ecclesiastical marriage laws which are demanded of couples in a parish setting (where many young people similarly fail to see the difference between a civil and a religious commitment). If one attempts to fully prepare couples in a parish setting by means of extended counselling sessions, so too, one attempts, against great odds, to do so in a setting of incarceration. Obviously, one has to compromise. Inmates headed from jail to prison oftentimes want to legitimize a longtime union which has produced offspring. They also wish to be allowed conjugal visits in prison, and wish, understandably, to bind their lovers to themselves in a legal commitment.

These weddings, when performed, are, by means of setting, sad; ugly experiences not only for the couples, but for any minister of religion who likes to make marriage ceremonies memorable for brides and grooms. They are generally performed in an office or consultation booth, over with in a few minutes; the couple newly united in marriage are almost immediately separated and he, she, or both are returned to the tier area.

Again, with no crystal ball, the chaplain has little way of knowing which marriages are made in heaven and which are done for momentary convenience or whim. Several days before I was to wed one prospective inmate groom to his fiancee from the streets, he was caught sodomizing a 16-year-old boy in the kitchen elevator (giving evidence perhaps that even the course of true love has its ups and downs). I ended up with egg on my face. He ended up with a 14-day lock in and no wedding until he graduated to the streets.

THE SOCIAL CHASM BETWEEN CHAPLAINS AND INMATES

Judging the representatives of mainline denominations to be ineffective in correctional facilities, Clemens Bartollas wrote:

> If any religion were acceptable, it would no doubt be of the sect and store front church variety, but institutional administrators tend to be adamant in their insistence on employing middle class chaplains to minister to primarily lower class offenders (in Bartollas and Miller, 1978:225).

Whether the immediate conversion sect and store-front variety of church would be effective with the wearying day-in, day-out work on facility tiers may be questioned. Nevertheless Bartollas correctly sizes up the imbalance. Those who choose to minister in facilities are usually ministering to people whose education and social background are very different from their own.

"The social chasm — black culture difference has been in prison for a long time," wrote one chaplain:

> Now Hispanic cultures add a different language plus many diverse cultures, e.g., Puerto Rican, Central American, Carribean. It is difficult to understand and feel. Also, the prison "pecking order." Values, culture and intellectual pursuits are a big problem. The impossibility to get "close to" as well as the non desirability of establishing close ties to a rapidly changing prisoner population is a big personal problem. Also, my interests do not coincide with many, e.g., who is top man, boxing, prison movies, to say nothing of pornography. I just don't relate at all to the interests for the most part (26).

One chaplain, meaning only to refer to inmates, said much about his own inability to span this chasm when he complained that:

> the ignorance of inmates in every facet of life is frustrating. Due to their ignorance they believe anything anyone tells them and do not have any ability to reason as to look at a situation logically. They do not know how to use information. they have no self-discipline and overreact to most situations. The hypocrisy and bullshit could build a mountain. They actually think we believe this nonsense (32).

Speaking more positively, another chaplain offered that: "at 46 I am painfully, on my own, learning Spanish, as 30% speak only this language" (39). Another suggested that a recent influx of Latin Americans involved not simply language problems but understanding as well the "drug culture" (42; Note 8).

Beyond any question of ethnic and cultural differences, the sensitivities which would lead one to become a minister of religion might further separate chaplains from inmates. If the former might tend to be "spiritual" and "other worldly" the latter tend to be, in large proportion, street savvy, hard realists who have learned to manipulate immediate situations to their practical advantage, and whose interests in the spiritual were well captured by the inmate, already quoted, who reflected about religious exercises: "You're supposed to meditate on God. Okay, you start meditating. I meditate for about five minutes and then I just get bored with it and I get up and start something" (Jackson and Christian, 1980:208).

Hugh Klare, in *Anatomy of a Prison*, wrote:

> There seem to be a few rare and saintly people whose personality and belief is such that they make a direct and sometimes lasting impact on many of those who lie in jail. But not all chaplains have this quality. At the same time a considerable number of recidivist prisoners are emotionally so shallow that to minister to their spiritual needs, to evoke some genuine response, must be heartbreakingly difficult (1960:79).

One reads repeatedly through literature which quotes inmates saying that the chaplain is often someone who "hellos" everyone constantly without ever getting into relevant conversation. The other side to this coin is that a chaplain of any sensitivity, working with inmates year in and year out, has to pretend to be interested in the conversational topics of the people Klare describes. When a chaplain encounters a truly educated, interested and literate inmate, sometimes that chaplain wouldn't care if that inmate were a Jack the Ripper; a visit to his cell would be looked forward to as an oasis of intelligent conversation. Even during a discussion of religion (as among those who want to discuss religion as a topic, not those who want religious consolation), such topics are most frequently of the "interpretation of the Book of Revelation" category (Note 9), and the theological level maintained is of the supermarket tabloid variety ("UFOs confirm; Jesus Visited Mars!").

Having seen both sides of the incarceration picture, first as an inmate and then as a social worker, John Irwin wrote in *The Jail* of the "have vs. have not" gulf which necessarily separates facility personnel from inmates:

> They must work closely with other humans (prisoners) who are in a state of deprivation and visibly suffering (If the deputies do not notice, the prisoners

will remind them). If the deputies remain committed to a philosophy of humanity and egalitarianism, or even to a basic sense of fairness, the plight of the needy and suffering around them will eventually take a heavy toll on their peace of mind and personal organization . . . I witnessed this process not only in deputies . . . but in myself and my fellow prisoner services caseworkers. We were constantly beseeched for more help than we could deliver, and we had to cope with feelings that we were not doing enough (one always knows that he can do more). In compensation for these feelings, we began to develop a more cynical view of our work and a more derogatory conception of the prisoner. We used the common term burnout to describe this process (1985:76).

As much as that may be true of deputies and social workers, it is certainly true of clergy, who, by profession, are called upon to be sensitive and caring. A social gulf can be felt on the occasions of having to tell inmates of deaths in their families. The gulf exists not so much because of the frequency of deaths which occur but the frequency of deaths owing to violence, and, in recent years, to AIDS.

Recently I was asked to tell a young female inmate of the death of her teenaged uncle. He was, in lived relationship, her stepbrother, for she had been raised by her grandmother. Her mother is presently doing time in a separate state facility than her daughter. The girl's uncle had been murdered; drowned in a bathtub. He had been living with a bullet lodged in his head, the result of a previous murder attempt following a bad drug deal. He had, in turn, stabbed his assailant in revenge, and the drowning was presumably a return attack.

The girl, though crushed by the news, had taken it well and sat quietly sobbing while an officer at whose desk we were sitting placed a call through to her grandmother. During the phone conversation she said: "Don't tell Raoul."

After she hung up she explained that he was her brother, doing time in Comstock. "Raoul doesn't take things well," she offered. After she left I said to the officer: "If just one of the things she mentioned in the past half an hour happened to you or me, we'd spend the rest of our lives referring to the great tragedy which occurred in our family."

One chaplain spoke of the frustration of "hearing of the abject poverty of spiritual direction, family crises, personal lack of self worth, lack of motivation for education and self improvement" balanced against his own "helplessness to change what's out on the streets." (14). Another spoke of endlessly hearing the "same stories and knowing what they need to do about it. But [I] can't find the resources to do it — with halfway houses, etc." (1).

Some inmates, reacting angrily to their situation, also take it out on the chaplain as a representative of the society of "haves," as noted by Rev. Joseph Sedlack, chaplain of Indiana State prison. "Some of them," said the priest, "use me as their whipping boy to rid themselves of their anger. Fact is, some of them even curse me" (Griswold et al., 1970:131).

At one point in the recent past, in Rensselaer County Jail (then at 125% capacity), this chaplain walked in to a top floor area, once used as a chapel, now used as a housing area. On a humid day, under a flat roof, inmates had been kept in extreme heat (above 90 degrees) for a number of hours without water or a toilet. The overcrowding, understaffing, and several incidents during the day had caused the prisoners to be forgotten. Understandably, they were forcefully angry, and took their anger out on me as if I had been the cause of their suffering. Somehow, as chaplain, I was expected to have an omniscience about what was happening in all corners of the facility. The principle and repeated theme of their tirade was that I was on one side of the bars and they were on the other, and that I should try getting on their side to develop some compassion for what they were going through. They did not need to hear excuses or an attempt at a rebuttal. I let them vent on me and then got an officer to attend to them. The stress I felt from their anger is part of the job.

Critics who feel that chaplains should share the same social background as inmates do not make the same criticism of other caring agents with respect to their clients (e.g., that a social worker must be homeless to effectively deal with the homeless). To rectify the matter, one might require that a newcomer to prison chaplaincy come from the ranks of the lower class, or be expected to broaden his/her perspective by knocking over a bank before entering this ministry; but, historically, some of the most effective people who have embraced social outcasts (e.g., Ghandi, Francis of Assisi, Mother Teresa) have come from the ranks of the middle and upper classes.

"RIDING THE RELIGIOUS PONY"

"Offenders are usually very pragmatic," wrote Frederick Wines. "They have lived in a world of facts, often very hard facts, and are apt to judge any teaching by its practical bearings" (1919:345). Prisoners tend to use this practicality in dealing with chaplains. Ironically, in this respect hostile inmates can be more refreshing than inmates who are aggressively friendly. Some of the more enduring friendships which I have developed with inmates — friendships which have endured beyond the time of incarceration — have been made with inmates who, at first, were hostile towards me. Their hostility was an indication that they wanted nothing from me. It is when a new inmate sits up fast on his bunk upon seeing me for the first time and says, "Oh Father, I was hoping the chaplain would stop by," that I brace myself for the ride.

As Rabbi Leibert observed, "every angle shooter has a softening up story." He continued: "I soon developed a conditioned reflex [so that] My mental guard went up automatically the moment a con approached me with the classic query, 'Do me a favor chaplain . . . ' I grew more wary as I became more familiar with the devious workings of the wayward mind" (in Leibert with Kingsberg, 1965:61). Leibert relates the story of an inmate working in a shop who made him a belt, a gift forbidden by prison rules. The chaplain agonized over the situation. Was he being set up or was the gift genuine, but misguided? After a sleepless night fretting out about what to do, he risked hurting the inmate's feelings and returned the gift (1965:195).

A friend of mine, Father Jim Hayes, is chaplain at Comstock Prison. A well-heeled inmate with underworld connections buttered Jim up for weeks. He finally insisted that Jim enjoy a trip to New York; the best of hotels, shows, it was all on the inmate's tab. When Jim delicately turned the offer down the man thereafter refused to speak to him. Had the man been disinterestedly sincere or was he setting Jim up? One doesn't know. Over the space of a number of years one finds out that he has been conned repeatedly, and each time a chaplain reaches a point where he feels that he has experienced it all and that he could never be conned again, he soon meets a clever confidence artist who is just a bit sharper than he is at the shell game.

The riding of the religious pony by inmates can cause no little bitterness in a chaplain. It is discouraging to buy an inmate's line about conversion, only to watch him drop that line when he hits the streets. The article written by Angola's inmates notes that:

> The total involvement of religionists and organizations with the inmate and all his problems has one drawback — one that everyone recognizes. It invites con and deception by insincere inmates hunting ways to secure their needs or obtain assistance in regaining their freedom . . . All the evangelists and religionists asked by *The Angolite* about the fakers admitted to having been stung and disappointed by someone they believed in who reverted back to crime after their release" (Rideau and Sinclair, 1981:50).

The question of "discovering that a trusted inmate has conned you for his/her own purposes," or, as one chaplain put it, the experience of "allowing inmates to 'get over' on me" (7) evidently concerns some chaplains deeply (Note 10). In the section defining chaplaincy one respondent had set up a picture of himself as a target to be conned, and he said, "I would clarify the position of a chaplain as viewed by many inmates. 'The chaplain has the juice,' 'Where's my free phone call,' 'I've got a problem which only you, chaplain, can help me with'" (14). One overworked target of such ploys wrote, "I feel a constant tension between (a) wanting to be open, loving and vulnerable to be a healing agent, and (b) being on guard against inmates' game playing and manipulation" (7). One perceptive chaplain touched a bit of salt to the wound in analyzing why "it is always troublesome to discover that you have been conned." "It is a matter of pride being hurt usually," he observed (12). *Touche.*

THE BURDEN OF CONFIDENCES

A staple in drama and fiction has been the situation of the clergyman who possesses confidential information about a crime but refuses to expose the criminal even when the law turns on the clergyman, himself or herself. Risking the displeasure of playwrights and novelists, chaplains survyed in this study agree that the problem of confidentiality is not a chronic concern in real life prison ministry (Note 11).

Nevertheless, a chaplain must always keep in mind that, if inmates within a facility ever become convinced that he or she informs the staff in any way about what is seen or heard on the tiers or about what is learned in private consultation, credibility and effectiveness will be completely destroyed.

Simply by observation, a chaplain discovers much which he or she might better not learn. The razor I found on a tier by chance is an example. It placed me in an uncomfortable quandary. Not wanting to be a party to any potential violence inflicted with such a weapon, I turned it in, and yet did so with no assurance of silence to the inmates. I do not want to be popular at the price of being a patsy. At the same time I staunchly refused to tell the administration which tier the razor had come from. Guarding is the guards' job, not mine, yet the incident left no one particularly happy with me.

That incident was momentary; another situation involving confidentiality lasted over weeks of time. Not long before this writing an undergraduate woman student disappeared from a local college campus. While the issue was still media spotlighted an inmate told me, in a confidential setting, that another inmate, incarcerated for a minor crime, had told him that he had killed the girl. He told me that her body had been put in a car trunk and dumped in the Hudson River. He added that he was himself desperately afraid of the other inmate because he possessed this information.

For days I was tortured with the burden of this revelation. It was a time when the girl's parents were being continually interviewed on the news. I felt a guilty, pressing responsibility to help, but was commanded to silence by my informant. The most I could do was to pressure him day by day to tell what he knew to someone whose role did not demand silence. I focused his attention on the girl's mother and insisted that he had a responsibility to her. Finally he told what he knew to an investigator. The alleged murderer denied his boast, and the lead to find the body led to nothing. Nevertheless, the incident is a classic example of the sort of pressure such confidentiality can place on a chaplain.

FAILURE AT REHABILITATION

"The infrequency of success stories in the after release lives of presumably rehabilitated inmates" is a statistic which some chaplains see as reflecting upon their own perceived lack of effectiveness. In the words of the chaplain of a women's prison, "the fact that so many return [gives evidence] that we are not really helping them"

(67). A county jail priest pointed out that "the constant flow of people into the system or returning to the system [creates] a lack of satisfaction [in] seeing results" (19 [Note 12]).

Chaplains walk this treadmill along with chronic repeaters. Two related entries made in my own diary/journal earlier this year, each written with the emotion as felt on the particular day bear witness to this:

1/15/92 — At about 8:30 this morning, shortly before I was to leave for the jail the phone rang. It was the Samaritan Hospital Detox unit. Joe H., who was about to be released, was asking for me. Would I come over and deal with the situation? I like Joe, but he is one of the world's aging flower children for whom time froze at Woodstock in the nineteen sixties. He looks like Charles Manson — without the insanity in his eyes, keeps his hair long and greasy, and his mind, whenever he can, blanked out on alcohol and drugs. His "woman" — if they are legally wed I don't know — is comatose in a nursing home in Arizona. In jail during December Joe had convinced me that I should find the means to get him back there to be with her. I really was going to do so, even if from my own funds; Joe and I go that far back in time. Constant idiot that I am I will now make sure I check out all income sources first. Joe got out of jail just in time for the January arrival of his $400 monthly disability check, which he proceeded to blow in one grand night, heralding the new year. This got him back into custody and into a fifteen day stay in detox.

I went to Samaritan and spent an hour getting him discharged. We left with Joe clutching a handful of prescriptions and appointment notices for his next stops on the social service circuit. We drove to a pharmacy in Lansing-burgh to pick up a leg brace, Joe having trashed his knee while celebrating. While there he had a couple of prescriptions filled, knowledgably directing the young pharmicist as to the mg. doses he wanted. As a ward of the state, he did all this handing pieces of paper over the counter rather than money.

We drove to his apartment. "Disabled" (how he's disabled I can't quite gather), Joe thus gets the apartment for $60 a month. It's not a bad little place except that he has trashed it. Rotting food lies all over the table and floor. Burnt out cigarettes dot the landscape wherever they landed after Joe flicked them away. When we entered the lights were burning as they had been for the previous two weeks.

"I always leave the lights on," Joe offered, with no further explanation.

When we left there I drove toward the St. Peter's Alcohol Rehabilitation Center where he had a 1 P.M. appointment. En route he snapped his fingers and declared that he had forgotten to open his mailbox: "I got a $250 check coming. It's a heat allotment."

He resisted being delivered to the center an hour early. Instead he wanted me to take him to Bethany [street person drop in] Center so he could check out which ones of his friends were there. I refused.

"But our appointment isn't til one o'clock," he objected.

"Joe," I corrected, "*Your* appointment is one o'clock. *I'm* going to work." I gave him McDonald's coupons for lunch [having learned to carry these for such situations in lieu of cash] reached over and opened the car door for him. As Joe pulled out his wallet to store the coupons he showed me a photo of his fourteen year old son, being raised by a sister-in-law.

"She couldn't have kids of her own so she went and stole mine," Joe said. This, finally, pissed me off. The boy in the photo looked well cared for and happy. Joe had walked away from him when he was an infant, and now he reasons that somehow, like everything else which is wrong with his life, it is all the fault of the world outside of himself. Because he is intelligent, and likeable, and because I've known him a long time I told him to cut the shit. He deserted the boy. Moreover, he could be out west now with his present woman if he had bought a bus ticket with his $400 disability check instead of blowing it all in one night. I told him that part of me would love to have a $400 a month income out of which I needed to pay only $60 in rent. I'd then get in line, pick up my food stamps for being a low income person, curl up in my apartment and live a pleasant "retired" existence.

For the entire day Joe was a frigging one-man industry for a sizable work force of people like myself whose employment was to take care of him. Goddamit, we've made "poverty" a demeaning system in this country; one which feeds the weaknesses of the Joes of this world and makes self destructive monsters of them.

I had to record a sequel to this entry on 3/10/92:

On the late Saturday news it was announced that the body of a man was fished out of the Hudson. As I listened to the description it snapped intuitively into my mind: "That's Joe." On the Sunday morning news the name was released. It was him. I guilt tripped. The last time I saw him was the day I chauffered him about after picking him up at the detox unit. He was an aggravation that day and I am sure that, while I did all the right things, I let him know by my terse demeanor that he was a pain in the ass. "If I give my body away to be burned but do it without love . . . "

IS THERE BURNOUT FROM OVERINVOLVEMENT?

One chaplain respondent who confessed to "not being able to get problems (jail) out of my mind when I'm off the job," and revealed that "the emotions that are directed toward me daily are almost too much to handle," said, "I sometimes feel like I'm trying to hold back a tidal wave" (40).

Michael Wolff, in *Prison*, describes the impact of a burnt out chaplain on a visitor who had just finished a six-hour tour of a "large central prison for long term prisoners:"

The whole place was, it seemed, being run like an efficient army camp, with prisoners going about their work with a will if not with a smile. Life did not seem too bad. At the end of the day came the visit to the chaplain. He described his work; then, quite suddenly he burst out: "But nothing that I can do can penetrate the atmosphere of evil that exists. You can have no conception of it." The chaplain may well have been exaggerating; after several years of trial and error, frustration and disappointment, he cannot be called on as a dispassionate, unbiased witness. Nevertheless, it was borne in upon the author that however much he might have been learning about the externals of prison life he knew little about the hearts and minds of the prisoners and their relations to themselves, to the staff and fellow prisoners, and to those outside (1967:17).

The article by Angola prisoners notes the workload pressed upon chaplains. The job is nearly infinite in potential. The problems are without end; one could listen to woes 24 hours a day and still not be on top of the job. As the inmates observe, some chaplains have been "forced out," others have "prostituted" themselves to the powers that be, while others "have sometimes valiantly, sometimes foolishly, jumped into the struggle to fight against a perceived wrong. They, as expected, bit the dust" (Rideau and Sinclair, 1981: 36).

Some go through a stage of burnout, and then come out the other side to be counted as survivors. Of these the inmates wrote:

There are some who are solid, realistic, cognizant of the various pressures and problems, and strive to strike that balance that will permit them to do as much good as possible . . . these are the ones who endure and prove most effective in their endeavors (Rideau and Sinclair, 1981:36).

Lionel Fox, noting that British Commissioners usually limit chaplains to seven years of service, relates that the commissioners believe that "a man who spends too many years in the highly specialized, difficult, and often discouraging work of a penal establishment tends to lose that spiritual zest, that freshness of touch which is essential in what must always be uphill work" (1952:90).

The chaplains in this study would seem to disagree with this. The dilemma of "being unable to emotionally draw back from the unrelieved problems of inmates" ranked low among their concerns (Note 13). Most chaplains acknowledged the presence of factors in their work which might cause stress, but at the same time they made it clear that they felt themselves capable of coping with these realities. Many of them refer to a mellowing, observed within themselves, over time. These chaplains who "endure and prove most effective" might well be listened to for advice in how to succeed in this difficult ministry.

NOTES

1. Both surveys of chaplains rated "the potential for danger" as being insignificant to them. The frequency mean was 2.3 in the State level survey; 2.2 in the Federal. The intensity of distress was a low 1.9 in the State level survey and 1.9 in the Federal.

2. "The possibility of contracting an illness such as AIDS or Hepatitis" rated low in both surveys; with respective frequency means of 2.2 and 2.1; and a distress level mean of 1.9 and 2.0.

3. The issue of "overcrowding, and the subsequent overloading of ministerial responsibilities" hit home as a distressing issue to the chaplains in both surveys. In the first almost two-thirds rated the experienced problem as 4-5 in frequency (with a mean of 3.5) and half adjudged it 4-5 in intensity (with a mean of 3.3). In the Federal survey it was again rated high, with 67.2% rating it a 4-5 in frequency (with a mean of 3.7) and 54.6% rating it 4- 5 in intensity (with a mean of 3.5).

4. The chaplains in both surveys ranked the item "invasion of inmate privacy when working on the tiers (toilet areas, etc.)" with moderately low respective frequency means of 2.6 and 2.4; and level of distress means of 2.0 and 2.1.

5. Ninety percent of the chaplains in the first survey rated "frustration about observed injustices within the criminal justice system" a 3-5 on the Likert scale for prevalence (with a 3.7 mean) and 87.1% rated it 3-5 in intensity of distress it produces for them (with a mean of 3.6). The Federal chaplains rated this item somewhat lower, 77.5% placing it in the 3-5 range of the prevalence scale (with a mean of 3.3) and 74.5% rating it 3-5 in intensity of distress (with a mean of 3.3).

6. The experience of "dealing with mentally ill inmates who should be in hospitals rather than in prisons" was rated moderately high in frequency (51.4% rating it 3-5 with a mean of 2.8), but higher in intensity of distress (57.1% rating it 3-5 with a mean of 2.9). Seventeen percent of the chaplains rated the encounter with imprisoned mentally ill offenders as a 5 in the intensity of distress it created for them. The Federal chaplains rated this item slightly lower, with a frequency mean of 2.5 and an intensity of distress mean of 2.7. One might conjecture that the higher rate in the first survey might be explained by the greater encounter with mentally ill inmates which one might expect to see in local facilities.

7. In the initial survey 81.4% of the chaplains rated the item of "dealing with inmates' family crises" 3-5 in frequency (with a mean of 3.3, while 70% rated it 3-5 in intensity of distress (with a mean of 3.0). and 34.3% rated it 4-5 as a distress factor. In the Federal survey 74.7% of the chaplains rated it 3-5 in frequency (with a mean of 3.1); 71.8 rated it a 3-5 in intensity of distress (with a mean of 3.1) and 44.6% rated it a 4-5 as a distress factor.

8. The item referring to "the social chasm which exists between most chaplains and inmates" was rated 2 or lower by 55.7% of the respondents (with a mean of 2.5), 64.3% scoring it low (2 or lower) on experienced discomfort (with a mean of 2.2). However, for the 20% who rated social distance a 4-5 on prevalence (11.4% rating it a 4-5 in discomfort), the problem, judging from the written comments, is felt sharply. In the Federal survey the means for frequency and intensity were slightly higher, respectively 2.7 and 2.5. By comparison 22.1% rated it 4-5 in prevalence (16.7% rating it a 4-5 in discomfort).

9. The issue of "hearing the same old stories over and over, told by inmates who fit very predictable patterns of behavior" was rated 3.3 in frequency of occurrence by the chaplains, 72.9% scoring it 3-5 on the Likert scale. At the same time the experience was rated lower in the intensity of distress it creates (44.3% rating it a 3-5 with a mean of 2.5). The Federal chaplains rated it 2.9 in frequency of occurrence, 67.8% scoring it 3-5 on the Likert scale. Likewise they rated it lower in intensity than frequency (48.5% rating it a 3-5 with a mean of 2.5).

10. Perhaps because of the touchy matter of pride more than half (54.3%) rated "being conned" a 3-5 in frequency (with a mean of 2.7) while two thirds rated it a 3-5 in discomfort (with a mean of 2.9). A comparable 54.2% of the Federal chaplains rated the item a 3-5 in frequency (with a mean of 2.7) as they showed themselves slightly less touchy, 49.1% rating it a 3-5 in discomfort (with a mean of 2.5).

11. The problem of "being burdened with confidences which should be known by authorities," was dismissed by the chaplains in the initial survey as only an occasional (mean 2.3) and relatively insignificant (2.3) experience within the ministry. None of the respondents elaborated on it as creating stress in their lives. The Federal chaplains concurred, again rating it a respective occurrence and discomfort mean of 2.3 and 2.3.

12. On the Likert scale, 71.5% of the chaplains rated lack of rehabilitative impact of their ministry 3-5 as to frequency of the experience (with a mean of 3.2) and 67.1% rated it 3-5 as to the intensity of the distress that disillusionment produces (with a mean of 3.0). The fact that the Federal chaplains would rate the item of recidivism lower (with a frequency mean of 2.7 and a distress mean of 2.6) might again be explained by the distance of the federal system from the streets, as opposed to the sometimes revolving door experience of local facilities.

13. The problem of being unable to emotionally draw back did not strike chaplains as very serious. Seventy percent of the respondents in the first survey rated it as occurring infrequently (2-3) — with a mean of 2.6, while 68.6% rated the problem a 2-3 in intensity of concern (with mean of 2.7). The Federal chaplains likewise rated the item low, with a frequency and intensity mean both measured at 2.5

Chapter 6

CHAPLAINS ON CHAPLAINCY

- "Go slow" (16).
- "It takes time (if it ever happens) to get used to jail or prison" (Campbell, 1989:44).
- "Prison and jail work is a long, slow process" (Pederson, 1979:83).

The first quotation is from a chaplain responding to this study. The next two, respectively, are from "manuals" on chaplaincy, one oriented to Catholics and the other to Protestants. Both books are excellently written and both offer wisdom and practicality borne of many years of ministry behind bars.

"I don't remember fearing for my safety in the prison [the first time entering]," recalls Sister Joan Campbell, S.P., in *The Ministry to the Imprisoned*, "as much as feeling powerless in the complexity of the system" (1987:17). Her words mirror those of the chaplains speaking through the survey. "I entered knowing nothing about it," offered one, "I was put in with no special training or orientation" (20). "I came with great fear . . . " admitted another, a chaplain at a maximum security facility (22). This writer/chaplain can offer the remembrance of my first few months in this ministry, oftentimes sitting in my parked car outside the jail, simply not wanting to go into the building and prolonging my entry for as long as I could.

Duane Pederson, in *How to Establish a Jail and Prison Ministry*, warns that, at first,

> you can expect to be overwhelmed, uneasy, and perhaps apprehensive . . . immediately struck with the pervasive security and regimentation . . . You will need to know the visiting hours and who can come and who cannot. You will need to know what, if anything, can be brought in to a prisoner. You will have to learn where you can go and where you cannot. You will learn about "the count," the periodic physical counting of all inmates at times during the day. The count is a fact of prison life that must be recognized and never interfered with. You have to plan your ministry efforts around it (1979:42).

Chaplains must walk carefully on eggs if they are to exist within the "Penitentiary" system which was, so ironically, created by their religious peers. Judging from what chaplains themselves say — e.g., "We try to fit in at the edges of spaces of the bureaucratic machine to find opportunities for creative work" (7) — one of the greatest challeges which exists for them on a day to day basis stems from a need of real communication between themselves and administrators of facilities. Moreover, as noted earlier, they often must work under administrators who think in terms of a secular programs model and who seem intent upon fitting chaplaincy work into such a "programs model" while chaplains, intent upon exercising a religious ministry, spend much energy in seeking to extricate themselves from, or to work through, such models. Both of the chaplaincy manuals mentioned earlier, addressing themselves to outsiders who would want to assist chaplains, point out that volunteers can be a boon to chaplains when such volunteers are consistent, dedicated and long range in their efforts. At the opposite end of the spectrum, those who show up for a short while so that they can tell "war stories," or who want to radically change the system, or who would ignore the inflexible rules under which this ministry must operate, become an added headache for the official chaplain.

"In some situations volunteers have bypassed the chaplain," observes Duane Pederson, "either to the prison administration or to the inmate, and the results has always been embarrassment, bad feelings, and a loss of stature for the religious ministry" (1979:61).

Sister Joan Campbell concurs: "Great harm can be done by a volunteer who fails to support the staff or who publicy rejects its authority" (1989:24). Both manuals agree that the primary purpose of security cannot be ignored and that "the first rule of prison ministry is *learn and follow all the rules*" (Pederson, 1979:42). Nothing, especially in the way of inmate communications, should be brought in or out of the facility. Patience with an inflexible system is a must. "I sometimes say I'd be rich if I had a penny for every minute I wait, " offers Sister Joan, "wait at the gates, wait for program and facility schedules, wait in the courtrooms, the attorney rooms and sometimes even to leave the facility" (1989:39). Nor can there be spiritual impatience, adds Pederson, quoting a chaplain who observes that "the ones who have failed have usually been those who try to 'hit the inmate over the head with the Bible'" (1979:77).

Again, "go slow." One cannot approach the task as if one were climbing onto a soapbox to give public witness at a busy intersection. We enter into a realm where "security" is boss.

It is interesting, and perhaps a bit confusing at first glance to the outside observer that in ranking the list of factors which they considered as stress factors chaplains in this study bypassed security concerns — such as "the potential for danger" which they ranked low — and ranked, instead, "injustices within the system" at the top of the list. Many of the chaplains strongly described their role in terms of being an advocate for the inmates. One chaplain wrote that chaplains are called to be "as clearly as possible a humane influence in a very brutal system . . . an advocate for human rights" (49). Many others specifically mentioned advocacy as a role of the chaplain and several expanded upon this point. That they did so was all the more significant in that the word was never used in the questionnaire sent to them, nor was there anything in the questionnaire overtly leading the chaplains to develop the concept so strongly as they did.

They did so on their own, emphasizing that "the chaplain is seen as an advocate; trustworthy and with some power" (13) or "preaching hope and [having] a rugged determination to 'fight the case' or to 'improve [the inmates'] condition,' to resist being downgraded" (60). "[You must have the] self confidence," declared a chaplain, "to face authority (security), to stand up for your convictions" (4).

Asked how he knew he was doing a good job, one respondent decided, "When I can feel the special pressure that comes from being on the fence; between the inmates and the administration" (30). "[The chaplain's] presence among the inmate population is vital in the safety and security of the institutions" (12), insisted one chaplain. Another captured precisely why this is so. Clergy, unlike others who work within the hidden world of facilities, are able to speak freely to a separate constituency on the outside. As he bluntly put it: "Chaplains are the only honest 'snitch' group in the organization" (19).

Both Pederson and Campbell warn against setting out to refashion the system as a whole. "If you want to work for prison reform, fine, " says Pederson, "But don't do it under the pretense of being a representative of Christ coming to care for inmates . . . Don't come in to tell the prison officials or the jailers how to do their jobs" (1979: 111, 83).

Sister Joan, citing that chaplains are "frequently in the middle of issues that lie between the incarcerated and 'the system, '" notes, at the same time, that most people are "unaware of the overwhelming complexity of the political, economic and sociological problems which have brought us to the unhumanness we see in the criminal justice system."

In other words, there are no simplistic solutions. If the system needs reworking — and it does — it cannot be initiated on the front lines where security problems exist. Philip Berrigan was angry because a chaplain would not melt the walls so that he could continue to meet, while incarcerated, with his fellow jailed protesters. This is not the kind of advocacy a chaplain can realistically pursue if he means to re-enter the building for work the next day. Instead, the chaplain must accept that he works in what Erving Goffman described as a "total institution." It is a society unto itself. It is within this harsh, totally enclosed society, dealing with corrections officers whose personal safety is also on the line, and dealing with top heavy bureaucracies (facility and governmental) that the chaplain must serve as an advocate.

In this reality advocacy often means struggling to see that things be done correctly according to the rules which the system itself calls for; to be a watchdog to see that easily ignored legal minimum standards be complied with. On a routine basis this involves hassles, sometimes major battles about matters which would seem miniscule to the public but which are at the heart of the reason why chaplains can say that their relationships with those in authority involve no little amount of tension.

David: Socks and Underwear

After 20 years of ministry to the incarcerated, I can measure the length of my career in time and observe that, every five years or so, I get into a confrontation with the authorities which threatens to end my career on the spot. It happened again earlier this year (1992) in an in-house, cold war style confrontation about socks and underwear. As recorded in my journal:

"David," now in his late twenties, had a black mother and White Father. He was abandoned and raised as an orphan. He is occasionally consumed by an anger against the world which is expressed in vandalism, most recently in the spray painting of the State Capitol building. He has been in jail many times.

Somewhere along the way David converted to Roman Catholicism and is rigorously conservative, frequently taking me to task for any "liberal" and non legal (canonically speaking) aberrations he sees in my chapel Liturgies. Somewhere along the way he also decided to become a "jailhouse lawyer," that breed of inmate who can and does keep administrators jumping by combing through minimum standard laws and complaining to the Commission of Corrections about failures of a facility to comply with specific regulations.

In the past few months David has been spending his days in the law library, digging out hidden legalities and lobbing them over the heads of the jail authorities and into the hands of the state commission. At first, he was laughed at and ignored, but as he continued pressing with his letters it became an increasingly common sight to see him in one of the glass consultation booths in the jail's main hallway intently telling a frustrated and defensive representative of the administration how to run the facility. He has won a series of decisions from the commission which have made everyone in the front office not only jump but tap dance continuously. A couple of examples:

David found that times for religious services are supposed to be posted on every tier. While on the tiers one day I was hailed by the public address system to the main offices. A desk job officer, clearly uncomfortable, asked me when we had religious services. I made the mistake of laughing.

"You don't know?" I asked incredulously. He was in charge of scheduling and services have been at the same time for many years.

The laugh was a mistake; it set the stage for the administrative wrath which was to ensue. David continued to issue complaints; about lists of potential visitors demanded by the jail, about who was allowed to leave the tier areas for programs and services, etc. The administrators were able to shoot him down on a few technical points, but he kept reformulating them and sending them right back. He pointed out the contradiction that some inmates are allowed to go to visits and the yard in the midst of general population and then told that they cannot go to religious services with the general population; and that an inmate who is to be separated from population for safety's sake is sometimes sent wandering alone through the hallways, guarded only by a slip of paper telling them to go to consultation, medical, etc.

The most incredible law which David unearthed was a forgotten WASP dictum dating to 1909. According to this New York State law, a Bible is to be placed in the cell of every inmate (we are, after all, conducting "Penitentiaries"). Amazingly, this statute was reaffirmed as late as 1951 — and still remains on the books. By this time the jail administrators were drawing their own six shooters — even as they continued to dance wildly at David's bidding. Hoping to appease his latest demand without calling on the state legislature to repeal the law they put several copies of the Bible in the library "accessible to all."

Then David found the law which would come close to destroying my career. He made and distributed copies of a minimum standard requirement stating that inmates were to be provided with footwear, socks, underwear, and sweaters. When he handed me my copy my jaw all but swept the floor in stupid surprise. It's about time that I became a jailhouse lawyer. I've been hustling to provide clothes for inmates for as long as I've been doing jails. Fool that I am for all these years, I never had to. I should have learned to read; it would have made life easier. I swore out loud at myself and congratulated David (a tactical mistake, for David referred to my congratulations in following through on the matter). The reaction of the administration, when David presented it to them as a demand, was to say that they would henceforth issue socks and underwear to any inmates who could prove that they were indigent. Drawn into the matter at this point, I offered my own correction. That is not the way the law reads. The law does not say "indigent." If Leona Helmsley were sent to us she would be entitled to jail issued underwear should she ask for it.

At this point the war began. The administration called for a chaplains' meeting, at which we were collectively accused of being the instigation behind David's campaign. No one who knew David — and they did — should have made such an accusation. He didn't need us for inspiration. When we were ordered to stick to preaching religion and to leave social issues to the social workers, I retorted — being the calm, cool person that I am, never given to excessive hyperbole — by telling the administration that they were bent on running a Nazi concentration camp. To my surprise, George Kalbaugh, the Episcopal priest, who really is calm and cool, broke out of his usual reserve and built upon my image of a Nazi camp. That is exactly what they are running, he agreed. They had just told us that we were to stick to theoretical religion and to close our eyes to physical conditions at the facility. "Just like Hitler wanted his chaplains to do, " he finished.

Three weeks later, on the last Monday in March, we were called in for another meeting. I don't know why God made me so naive. I honestly anticipated that they wanted to know what we were doing with Easter Services. Instead, a promulgation was read to us. For reasons of security the chaplains, from this point in time, were no longer to be allowed to go back to the housing areas. If any inmate wanted to see a chaplain he/she could fill out a form [at this point we were handed the form] to be sent through the inmate service unit for approval. We could then meet with such individuals in the lawyer's consultation booths. I sat in shock. Before I could react enough to get hot-headed, George stood up and handed the form back. "This will fall of its own weight, " he said. He turned to the rest of us chaplains and said, "I think that we should repair to a diner and conduct our own meeting." Without further comment we walked out. I was still too dumbfounded to talk.

Over coffee, George suggested that we play the victims of policy, letting the inmates react to the situation. We had been told by the administration that, coinciding with our being called to the office, a copy of this new rule had been posted on every tier. If we were going to tell our side of the story it would have to wait until weekend services where, no doubt, what we said would be monitored by the administration. By Thursday morning my dumbfoundedness had worn off.

After teaching my morning class at Siena College, my workaholism kicked in. I had nowhere to go; nothing to do. I was off my programmed schedule. Sharing the situation with Ned McGlynn, chair of the Sociology Department, I said, "I literally don't know what to do with myself." I drove to the jail knowing that none of the new forms would have appeared yet in my mailbox.

The situation was too confusing and inmates would not yet understand what was transpiring. As I anticipated, there was nothing for me to do at the facility. My hands were tied.

As I later found out, things I would have looked after fell by the wayside. The day I was told not to return to the tiers I had brought a suit into the facility, given to me by the mother of a young man going to court. I had then handed the suit to a staff person who promised to get the suit to him. He never got it; he went to court in his green jail jump suit. On another tier, a middle-aged man's father had died suddenly (in Connecticut). The message, sent in to the facility by the family, died with the officer at the end of the tier, who, for whatever reason, did not tell the man at the time and then forgot about it. When the man accidentally called home the bereaving family found out that he had never been told. There was deep, understandable anger. There was no way for me to initiate any kind of attempted healing presence into the situation.

A Waiting Game

I left the jail that Thursday morning and sat in my car — upset — realizing that I was cut off from living out my ministry. Impulsively, I snapped off the ignition, went back into the building and upstairs to the front offices. I asked the Superintendent's secretary if I could see him. Evidently not aware of the situation, she was friendly to the point of effusiveness. In a moment she returned with a friendly, apologetic:

"Father, he's busy right now.

"I'll wait, " I said.

She went in and came back out, the smile gone now.

"He's *very busy*, Father.

"Tell him I'll wait, " I said, tersely.

I went out into the main hallway and stood. Politely she came out and asked if she could get me a chair. I declined the offer. Eventually I sat on some piled boxes of copier paper. It was ten in the morning when I started waiting. At noon, engineers for some ongoing construction entered the office. In a few moments the Superintendent went out with them, passing by without acknowledging my presence. The secretary came over to me and very apologetically told me that he was out to lunch. I said I would wait.

Shortly after one in the afternoon he returned. After a few moments the secretary came out and told me: "Father, he says that he is going to be blocked in all afternoon."

"Tell him, " I said, "I will wait until five o'clock when he goes. And if he cannot see me I will be back tomorrow morning at eight to continue waiting."

Another hour passed. The atmosphere around the front offices had grown tense. All secretarial and clerical bantering ceased. Officers wandered up the stairs, occasionally coming over to attempt to engage me in conversation. I was tightlipped and monosyllabic in response. Occasionally someone would enter a cubicle and I would hear a whispered: "What the hell is going on?"

It was arguably the most productive paperwork day the place had ever known. No one looked up from their work. No one went to the bathroom. They had to go past me to get there.

I repeatedly said the Rosary in order to keep myself in a state of calm. At 2:20 the secretary came out and said that the Superintendent would see me. I went in to his office and said as evenly as I could:

"I want to talk about the new ruling . . . "

He put both hands up as if I had surprised him. "I won't talk about that without the rest of the staff being here, " he said.

I said nothing. I didn't move a face muscle. He got up, went to his secretary and told her to round up the staff. Coming back, he sat down, smiled and asked: "What do you think about the construction?"

"I don't want to talk about the construction, " I said.

For several long minutes we sat in awkward silence while, one by one, officer and civilian staff officials filtered in, obviously pre-informed about the situation. No one said a word.

The Superintendent finally gave me the floor and told me that I could speak as long as I wished without interruption. If I checked my watch correctly afterwards I spoke for an hour and twenty minutes. I kept my voice even and calm as I attempted to explain the necessity of chaplaincy. At one point I nearly lost my cool when I used the word "evil" to describe the present situation and one officer, his voice raised angrily, jumped in with the demand: "Are you saying that I'm evil?"

I actually prayed myself down from the anger I felt ("Keep me calm, God . . . "), and answered, "I said the situation was evil." The same officer started to wax on about security needs. I reminded him that it has been a number of years since he graduated from tier work to the front offices. He doesn't walk the housing areas of the jail. I do. "I could take you back there right now and point out 20 immediate security breaches which would look incredible if they were presented to the local media," I offered. The threat was veiled and remained so. "Chaplains are the only honest 'snitch' group in the organization."

Rapid Response

As I was to find out later, the phone wires between the jail and the downtown political organization had been alive all day long. The incident had the potential for being a media sideshow if any one of us was to break through a sense of reserve and go public. I held to the Nazi simile, suggesting that if the jail wanted to find a particular precedent for their ruling, they might find an unusual case here and there in the history of the United States, but for a general precedent in barring clergy from prison work they would indeed have to look to places like Nazi Germany or the Communist Soviet Union. I ended with one story about the importance of chaplaincy presence on the tiers, pointing out I have the date of the incident recorded in my journal and could verify the incident from the jail's medical log if it had to be checked.

Several years earlier, doing my rounds I walked onto the second west tier one day and a boy, sweeping the floor, dropped his broom, rushed to me, burst into tears, and shoved into my hands a bloody pair of underpants. "They raped me, " he sobbed, turning and pointing to two older men who sat at a table glaring back at us. It was a dangerous situation. We were all locked in together. He was on the other side of the cat walk bars from me, in with them. They had heard his accusation. The boy had been as afraid of the particular officer on the tier as he was of his assailants. He had been waiting for me to come on the tier.

"Come with me, " I said. At the end of the tier I took the phone, got the Captain's office and said: "I want someone to come here and take this boy from this tier as I leave it. No questions." Finishing my plea for chaplaincy I threatened as mildly as I could: "If you take me off the tiers using security as a reason, that's the documented story that I will use as my defense."

The Superintendent made a wise move, for we had all moved into position for a High Noon showdown. He said that he wanted to say nothing at the moment. He wanted to think about things for a day. The next day, Friday, I received a call. The order had been rescinded. The Superintendent had been doubly wise to end the situation before the weekend. Given the penchant of some inmates for drama we might have ended up playing the "sit-in" game in chapel. I just breathed a sigh of relief and made the resolve to play very small for awhile; no victory. Business back to usual. On Monday morning the Superintendent called me to his office.

Once, years ago when he was still a tier officer, I had lent him my own Communion pyx so that he could bring the Eucharist each day to his dying father. His climb into authority had separated us from an easy give and take and we had not talked in a long time. We did so now. A calm assessment after a storm. Socks and underwear. As items they don't carry the high media profile won by nuclear plants when spray painted by protesters, but in the give and take world of chaplaincy, they spell *Advocacy*.

Unique Satisfactions in the Chaplaincy

Asked what they found uniquely satisfying about their unusual ministry chaplains repeatedly expressed what might be called a sense of the "heroic" about their labors in what one called "mission territory" (38), ministering in a setting where, "in spite of the overwhelming injustices and negativity of the environment, sharing the journey of personal change with an inmate is most gratifying" (4). One chaplain described his work as "reaching out to those who are the most abhorred by society" (15). Another referred to "the near total dependance on the chaplain to stand up for these men — and when you win them a right denied, there is a personal satisfaction of David defeating Goliath again" (35).

Little wonder that Duane Pederson decided that while "chaplains work long hours under difficult conditions, dealing with personal crises of inmates every day" they must do so while "fighting the frustrations and disappointments that are an integral part of the prison chaplaincy" (1979:59). Sister Joan Campbell observes: "This is a ministry calling for patience, adaptability, and the ability to cope with the stresses of the corrections system and the issues of the incarcerated . . . Because of confidentiality within the facility and on the outside, the chaplaincy role is unique and one frequently feels like no one understands . . . It is not necessarily a popular ministry even within the Church" (1989:34).

ISOLATION

Even when a chaplain is blessed with good volunteer help, his or her role within the facility is ultimately that of a spiritual lone ranger. Despite the sometimes presence of volunteers, and presuming that the chaplain works well with chaplains of other faith groups, each chaplain is generally the sole official representative of his/her denomination. While officers and other staff members have the opportunity of gathering in groups of peers, the chaplain essentially works alone. It is thus understandable that, in answering the question, "to whom do you turn for spiritual and professional direction in dealing with your ministry," few of the chaplains responded to the phrase "professional direction." The few who did so mentioned direction within the facility: e.g., "administration" (28), "on occasion the deputy Superintendent of programs" (15), "psychologist at prison, and medical staff also, and teachers" (39).

None of the chaplains mentioned his or her denomination as having provided any kind of direction for the ministry — a glaring lack which ties in with the historic portrait of denominational neglect of chaplaincy, and the attitude, so constantly attested to, of historic abandonment by churches of those who enter this hidden world. In the absence of direct training or guidance from their denominations, many chaplains, after they are on the job, discover networks of support — often encountered in mailed flyers addressed to the "Chaplain" at a facility. These networks take the form of voluntary associations such as the American Correctional Chaplains' Association, and similar organizations specialized according to denomination. The general lack of official support from faith groups makes it unsurprising that many chaplains insisted that denominations should set up training programs and support groups for those who enter into jail and prison ministry.

Nevertheless, the sense of feeling isolated was rated low as a stress factor in the survey's Likert scale. Presumably people who opt to work in a ministry, which is by definition separated from the community at large, measure their own personality needs in accepting the work. Some of the chaplains left blank the space provided after the question "to whom do you turn . . . ?" Many of the respondents mentioned their fellow chaplains as persons with whom they shared. A small number of respondents answered "no one" or "no one in particular." A check of the questionnaires showed that these respondents did not assign themselves discomfort levels any higher then those who sought support from others. With one or two exceptions, the Likert scale ratings by those who listed support from others and those who did not indicate that being a loner does not necessarily denote loneliness in chaplaincy.

Working with a congregation in a second ministry away from the facility showed itself to be a something of a "wildcard" issue. While some clergy decried having to do double duty — "I'm returning to a very busy parish. Two jobs!" said 60 — others found prison chaplaincy to be a welcome escape from the politics and administrative tasks of a congregation, and still others found their congregations to be a saving grace from prison pressures (Note 1), "Returning to the parish and being involved there helps me," wrote one chaplain (61). Another testified: "I find my parish very relaxing. Working with these people is a real joy" (32). The suggestion to involve oneself with a congregation outside the facility was at times tied to spiritual needs: e.g., that chaplains need an "outside Faith Community to become involved in, not necessarily ministerially" (17).

A chaplain serving at a medium security, Federal prison reinforced this, advising: "Be active in local church, as parishioner with family" (39). The only absolute warning against a second ministry came with the qualification that each role not be considered a full time position — "Don't try to pastor full time and be full time chaplain; one area will suffer" (2).

RELATIONSHIPS WITH INMATES

Neither Sister Joan nor Duane Pederson, as devoted as they are to inmates, romanticize about them in order to sound like proper "dogooders."

"Some will completely reject you, curse you, and want to have nothing to do to you," warns Pederson, adding:

> Others will try to use the relationship with you to further their own ends. Inmates tend to look for what they can get immediately and they often see other people as objects to be used, much as they themselves have been used. Their attitude may be, "What can you do for me today?" Even God and religion are considered things to be manipulated. Many chaplains can tell of

"thirty-day conversions" — inmates [who] try to use the language of faith and prayer, then reject God and the Bible because they get no results (1979:71).

"Most of their previous relationships have been built on using others and being used, " agrees Sister Joan. "Do not be surprised if they try some of this manipulation on you" (1979:27).

The whole context of ministry must be kept in mind when considering statements made by chaplains on this point. Quoted out of context they would seem a denial of mission.

- "Do not get emotionally involved with inmates" (32) advised one Catholic chaplain, with a Protestant chaplain adding, "If you find yourself feeling sorry for an inmate watch out. If necessary, discuss it with someone" (7).

- Concurred an Imam, "I would caution him/her [a chaplaincy newcomer] not to allow himself to become totally giving, to always be willing to step back and take a look at the whole spectrum of his frame of work" (47).

- A Rabbi at a metropolitan jail advises chaplains to "recognize that what you see may not be what it is since you know nothing of inmates before incarceration" (58).

- "I would clarify the position of a chaplain as viewed by many inmates, " offered a minister serving at a medium security state facility, " — 'the chaplain has the juice,' 'Where's my free phone call?' 'I've got a problem which only you, chaplain, can help me with.' These are manipulative statements and one must see through them" (14).

At this point one might ask: If all this is so, then why would anybody want to go into chaplaincy? The first answer is that God demands it. A person responding to a need for chaplains might not feel a particular "calling" to it, but may realize that it is simply a job which must be done, and that God wants it done. The Sacred Scriptures of all faith groups make it clear that God, with a judging eye, watches how the world treats prisoners. "Be mindful of prisoners as if sharing their imprisonment, " admonishes the Epistle to the Hebrews (13:3).

Many of the contributing chaplains, giving the reason for their entry into this ministry, cited Chapter XXV of the Gospel of Saint Matthew as the "scriptural basis of the ministry." In this passage, which enumerates physical works of mercy, Jesus says: "I was in prison and you visited me." When it is asked of him, "When did we see you in Prison?" he responds: "I say to you, whatever you did for one of these least brethren of mine, you did for me." Aside from the clear demand of God there is the realization that prison ministry is necessary because human beings are in need. In the words of one chaplain, "The suffering is acute and universal. Each minister is so needed. I feel that I am really using my time to alleviate pain" (66).

Perhaps most importantly, beyond any sense of duty, chaplains indicate that, with time and a maturing in their own chaplaincy, they experience a growing sense of genuine, personal, and individual love for prisoners. One chaplain declared that she came to prison "to bring God's love to people in a very harsh setting" (2). It is a love which ceases to see prisoners as a collectivity. Each one of them is valued and loved as they are loved by God. "I thought I'd be dealing with dangerous people," wrote the chaplain of a maximum security prison, "They're really overgrown teenagers who have to hear the word 'no.'" He adds, "I feel I am their father they never had" (45). A woman chaplain at a medium security facility shared that, for her, ministry "means loneliness often, and endurance always. It means interpreting the 'Good News' in practical gestures — like phone calls — and not minding not being very popular sometimes. It means loving and loving and being a mother and a father to lots of little boys and girls" (4). Another maximum security chaplain agreed that he, too, came "with great fear" of dangerous inmates, but learned "that they are as human as ourselves. Some of them are so good. Circumstances have made them criminals" (22).

Although a few chaplains might define their role in purely religious and even exclusivist terms — e.g., "Bible studies and prayer services should be made available and mandatory in *all* facilities" (6) — most chaplains recognize that their presence on the tiers means that they must respond, as well, to the inmates' emotional and physical needs on a number of corresponding levels. One minister observed that chaplains should be skilled in "Counseling in many areas (religious, social, future, drug, chemical addiction); adapting to many cultures, worship formats. Sensitivity to needs, i.e., anger, guilt, disease" (15).

Maintaining a sense of balance is advised. One chaplain who described his role strongly in terms of advocacy also said: "Worship should be a highlight of an inmate's week. It can help him/her through terrible times" (13). Conversely, one who began by quoting Matthew 25 stipulated, as well, that every chaplain should have a "background knowledge of Criminal Justice System" (64).

One minister advised his peers to be "first of all well grounded in the Bible; secondly, in the field of psychology; and thirdly, in the necessary rules and procedures of the particular part of the correctional system in which you do your task" (5).

A woman minister opined that an ideal chaplain would be "professionally trained in clinical counseling and/or psychotherapy; committed to the covenant that what we do to the least is required by God; [with] administrative abilities; sensitive but not gullible" (2). One priest, serving at a medium security facility, interjected: "Love yourself. Take care of you — so you can love others" (16). This call to inner peace, inner acceptance is essential. Throughout all the responses was a permeating realization that chaplains must be authentic. They must be themselves; be honest about their own frailties and vulneribilities, and convey this honesty in their relationships with prisoners. We cannot give what we do not have. We must always be striving for a sense of holistic spiritual and emotional well-being for ourselves if we are to bring it to prisoners on the tiers.

In describing their role on the tiers many of the chaplains continually used words such as "presence" and "availability." A chaplain cannot be effective in prison without being immersed in it. "Visit; make rounds often. Be visible and listen. Be dependable and accountable," (13) offered one. Another insisted: "You must change schedules often to be of help to the inmates. Their level of tolerance is not good, so they want to 'talk' when they are ready" (55).

Even entering into what may be, at first, an alien culture for a particular chaplain, honesty and openness, a genuine interest in each individual as an individual, and the ability to listen with undivided personal interest will bridge every cultural gap. "Learn to accept people as they are," advised one priest. "Don't try for too many changes. One has to adapt to cultures, life experiences and a rough, violent existence" (26). Another insisted upon the development of "good listening techniques," along with "availability throughout the institution, especially in the 'closed' or locked down areas" (42). "Be willing to listen — even though the same story might be heard ten times a day," (44) put in another chaplain, which yet another qualified as "listening with the ears and heart — counseling — healing through presence and words and touch" (17).

Given this realization of the importance of interpersonal relationships, it is little wonder that, when asked how they know when they are doing a good job, the majority of the respondents agreed with the chaplain who gave the common sense reply, "First, ask the inmates" (12). As another chaplain noted: "Inmates are very good at letting you know" (29). Other chaplains qualified this concept: "A good barometer," decided one, is "how many inmates come to talk and ask no favors" (33). "I know I am doing a good job," said another, "when inmates communicate with me on a one to one basis for long term direction and counseling. This is happening as inmates consider me to be a teacher, a carer, a helper" (14).

"The lives of a few inmates who are now productive citizens, married, staying out of trouble and who are in contact with me regularly" (52) was cited by one chaplain as a long range measurement, while another looked at a shorter range of time, — "When inmates, in small ways, start taking responsibility for their lives and actions" (41). On this idea of knowing when they have done a good job a few of the chaplains pointed out, rightly, that measurable success is somewhat beside the point in assessing one's mission.

"If I am here it is good," said one, adding, "Success at best is a fleeting concept" (26). Another wrote that "I would measure success by the amount of myself I put into what I was doing, not on the number of people responding" (20). A third decided that, from the vantage point of faith, the matter was ineffable. "There is no human evaluation form," he said, "I get a night's rest. God does the bookkeeping, if any is done" (37).

THE GRAYING OF CHAPLAINS

The chaplains who contributed to this study were older in experience than the average chaplain in the field. Unlike those who might enter chaplaincy and wash out, they have weathered the shock experience of getting used to the prison world, have oftentimes gone through the process popularly labelled "burnout" and have emerged on the other side into a deeper acceptance of their role. Acquired flexibility seems to be the key. "Be open to growth and continual appraisal," advised one," . . . [insofar] as a chaplain is functioning in a very compressed, simplistic, stressful environment" (14). In being flexible, they attest that, with the passing of years a mellowing and acceptance process sets in, directed toward oneself, toward inmates, and toward those with whom one worked in the facility. "Go slow" remains the initial advice to fiery zealots, newly arriving upon the scene (16).

Acceptance of self was the subject of several responses. "The older I get and the longer I stay at the same prison," wrote one chaplain, "the better the ministry trust level" (39). Another admitted: "I can't change as much as I thought" (40). It was an admission made by many of the chaplains in like-phrased statements. Others offered that experience had made them more philosophical about being misused.

"I have a better idea of who is conning me now," said one, "but it really doesn't matter very much" (66). Acceptance of officers and staff members was emphasized by other respondents. As quoted in the section dealing with COs, chaplains developed, with years of experience, a continually deepening respect for the officers with whom they worked over the years, worrying about their well-being and about the strain which their jobs place upon them and their family relationships, etc.

There was one area wherein chaplains showed no mellowing. Consistent with the high Likert scale rating about frustration felt about injustices within the system, chaplains wrote that years of experience only sharpened such frustration. The chaplain who spoke of a growing respect for officers also wrote that "I am more convinced of the wastefulness of human life due to overlong sentences and virtually no allowance for alternatives to incarceration" (42).

"I can't change as much as I thought," said another chaplain, but added that "I have to accept more things I don't like than I thought I would" (40). A third chaplain said that "The Church is in the prison not just for the 'service and maintenance' of inmates, but also to watch the government lest it sin worse than the inmates" (60).

The chaplains contributing to the study made it clear that the stresses they felt were not great enough to run them aground in their work. They indicated that stress is a natural part of their job. One chaplain noted: "The issue of stress is very real. Every ministry encounters stress, and suggestions about creative management of it are always welcome. [But] if we become successful in elimination of stress, I feel that we will have eliminated any effective ministry. Pursuit of effectiveness is stress producing" (12). Another chaplain commented on the Likert scale: "The demands above are low keyed and not large distress factors. Anyone in above who moves 4-5 consistently does not belong in prison chaplaincy" (44). In one respect the contributors to the study proved the opposite of what was anticipated. The Likert scale questions were designed to measure the frequency and intensity of distress factors in chaplaincy. Instead of taking the offered lead and using the questionnaire as an opportunity to dramatize their ministry or grouse about difficulties they encounter, the chaplains rated most of the Likert scale items only moderate levels with regard to both these aspects of potential discomfort.

On the contrary, what came through, in a very positive sense, is that, without boasting, the chaplains who responded to the questionnaire see themselves as tough and resilient individuals. They feel they can bear the burdens of others; they were given the strong shoulders to do so. This self-defined toughness is not toughness in any macho sense of the word. Chaplains see their own vulnerability and the dangers of giving in to situations which could cause undue stress. That is why the most valuable contribution that this study could make includes the chaplains' awareness of these dangers and, as phrased by the chaplain above, the corresponding "suggestions about the creative management of it."

Some of the advice given about relationships with inmates might offer scandal to dewy eyed idealists. For example, chaplains do not lose sight of the fact that they are dealing "with people who have little means to help themselves, who often have given up hope, do not have anyone who is ready to listen to them" (52). Yet, a not untypical piece of advice was: "Don't give inmates your home phone number or encourage them to call you" (66). The wisdom of this was learned the hard way by the aforementioned protest group who encouraged inmates to call and who finally ended up getting an unlisted number.

The problems are never-ending; so are the pleas for help. It is not unusual for families, even loving families, to put blocks on their phones to discourage endless collect calls from tier end phones.

One chaplain had said that he enjoyed inmates more than his outside parishioners because they were "more honest once past initial con" (62). This realistic and nicely balanced statement should be kept in mind in listening to the advice of those experienced in dealing with the "initial con." "Check out what inmates tell you before acting on it," concluded another, suggesting, "Don't promise what you cannot deliver" (35). Yet another repeated the point: "Make no promises to inmates. Do your best but rely on God to do it all. And have a sense of humor" (69).

The idea of not promising what cannot be delivered was ageed upon by many chaplains. It is a matter of the careful weighing of resources, including one's own capabilities. "Don't allow yourself to be trapped into overextension" (12) warned one. Others agreed, saying, "avoid the excessive multiplication of programs whereby none can be carried to complete fruition" (23). "Establish a routine and try to stick to it. Be satisfied to do what you can do" (7).

"All of the work that needs to be done will not be done by one alone," opined a priest at a large metropolitan jail. "There are succeeding generations . . . The individual chaplain will do what he can to lessen pain and suffering, his own as well as that of others, without feeling defeated in an imperfect society" (65).

"Don't be the 'saviour of the world' — do the best you can — even if it is just for one person a day," was a response typical of many. Another noted that "the work depends on God, not me. [I can] feel with inmates, but their problems are not mine. [Keep a] sense of humor. Don't take [your]self too seriously" (62).

The reminder to "have a sense of humor" reappeared constantly throughout the responses, almost as if it were the ultimate key to successfully coping with a stressful ministry.

THE "CREATIVE MANAGEMENT" OF STRESS FACTORS

One chaplain wrote that she had learned to "always allow for a break during the day in which you do something different; play cards, read a novel, do a crossword puzzle. Know your own limitations; don't allow yourself to be pushed beyond them" (4). However they may pace themselves while on the job, the chaplains almost uniformly agreed that at the end of the day's work it was important to walk out of the facility and consciously "turn it off" (66).

A sampling of views includes statements such as "I try to be away from the facility two days a week . . . Not being there is essential to being there" (26) and "I simply do not bring work home, and do not use the home phone for business" (25).

Prison life is extremely noisy. The constant yelling, clanging of metal gates, televisions and radios turned up full blast, blaring and echoing off concrete and steel; none of this is conducive to peace of mind. Sometimes, especially in winter when closed windows make this din seem all the more piercing, this writer/chaplain will leave the facility and stand on the front steps for a long moment allowing himself to be engulfed by the sudden rush of silence (Note 2). One chaplain wrote:

> I take a deep breath when I walk out of the facility. I tell myself that just as I'm exchanging the air in my lungs, I'm exchanging the emotions from inside with the concerns to outside prison life. I also have alone time when I'm driving (10).

Commuting a substantial distance was seen as a decompression opportunity by a number of chaplains — "meditate as I drive my 45 minutes home" (6) or "During my 1 1/4 hour one way commute, I pray the rosary and listen to the radio" (67) or "During my long drive home, listen to worshipful Christian music and begin to worship the Lord" (59) or "a half-hour drive home listening to an all sports radio station from New York City" (31).

Others added a wide range of pastimes and hobbies as means of decompressing; from music, gardening, cooking, and "quiet time" to social activities with friends and with organized groups and clubs. Interestingly, because the chaplains surveyed were not exactly a bunch of kids in linear age, physical exercise, often strenuous exercise, was mentioned as a decompression technique. Running, skiing, biking, racquetball, and swimming were balanced with walking, fishing, golf, and the supine exercise of one respondent who suggested "a monthly, full body professional massage," adding, "Try it. You'll like it!" (7). One chaplain, describing techniques for decompression, offered a touchingly personal note. He warned: "Don't drink to unwind; too dangerous" (39).

Chaplains cited the absolute necessity of relying upon a network of support from those they love. Many of the respondents mentioned their fellow chaplains as persons to whom they turned for companionship. Some spoke of their reliance on other priests, ministers, sisters or "colleagues," or of a spiritual director. Family and friends were repeatedly spoken of as strength givers, friends often being qualified as "spiritual friends" (4) or "friends who share my value system" (19). Socializing is seen as a necessity for emotional well-being, attested to by a number of the references made by the respondents:

- "Usually I can leave it behind, but if I am especially 'riled,' I take a walk or talk about it with someone" (21).
- "Usually my wife and I 'talk down' the day and let it all go" (13).
- "Good friends; celebrations" (16).
- "Visit fancy restaurant weekly and have weekly staff meetings at local restaurant to relax and break bread together with staff and volunteers and retired chaplains. Meet with area clergy for lunch; train clergy as volunteers" (39).
- "Get involved with ordinary people" (29). "I have a good friend who is skilled in listening" (68).
- "My social relationships in the neighborhood" (22).
- "I celebrate a liturgy at a local church and have dinner with the pastor. I find it refreshing" (20).

The deep spirituality of the chaplains permeated their answers, and their relationship with God underscored many of their responses about themselves. They became more explicit when asked about advice they would give to newcomers. "Above all, have a DAILY, PERSONAL, BIBLICALLY-BASED PRAYER LIFE!," admonished one chaplain (emphasis his) describing this as, "reflection on the *now* with God's presence" (19). Throughout the survey responses prayer was often mentioned in conjunction with another activity, as if it were as much a part of life as the air that is breathed. At one point or another a prayerful relationship with God was usually mentioned as a source of strength and in an offhanded manner that seems to say that this should be taken for granted — "Naturally, I turn to God" (15). Usually just the word "Prayer" was mentioned; often "Prayer and . . . " Occasionally this is expanded: "Write prayer journal" (39); "Prayer groups" (16); "If I need 'decompression' during the work day I go to our chapel and just sit quiet with the Lord for a few minutes" (21); or simply, "I trust in the Lord" (66).

A WORD TO THE OFFICIALS RUNNING THE SYSTEM

At a state level chaplain's conference which I recently attended, a young priest new to prison ministry stood up and said that he found himself overwhelmed by the irrelevant and time consuming amount of paperwork demanded of him by the programs director at his facility. He asked the rest of us how we managed to handle it. There was a pause. Then an older priest, a full-faced, white-haired, professorial sort of fellow who had the look of a Gilbert Keith

Chesterton, took the floor. "Screw it up!" he commanded authoritatively. The entire gathering erupted in laughter. Warming to this he expanded upon the suggestion. "I mean, do it with class; we all know how to do it with class — but screw it up! When the programs director tries to pile paperwork on me I go back to him with so many questions and interruptions he wishes he'd never come to work that day."

It was yet another communal realization that chaplains and administrators often fail to communicate, and that when they attempt to do so they are often at cross purposes, talking pears and bananas. Bureaucrats are intent upon making chaplaincy fit into a programs model and chaplains are intent upon ministering with an understanding of one on one confidentiality. Politicians fluctuate back and forth, sometimes treating chaplaincy as a sacred cow and at other times as a sitting duck.

In other words they will routinely turn their back on examining the workings of chaplaincy in ordinary times, as if they were too polite to question the doings of the clergy. By doing this they allow for inequities in expectations and in quality of performance. Then, in times of budget crunches, they reach out blindly to knock off chaplaincy as if it were an appendage to the system, without ever examining its actual value. One surprising fact which surfaced from the survey, one which says much about bureaucratic confusion with regards chaplaincy, was the presence of some chaplains working full time in small facilities, and some chaplains working very few hours in some of the largest facilities.

To clarify this situation, a cross tabulation on the survey returns was run, separating the chaplains by the percentage of weekly schedule spent in the facility and the size of the facilities. No consistency seems to exist with regard to full- or part-time employment policies for chaplaincies on the part of varying facilities. Several of the respondents worked less than 20% of a weekly schedule in facilities with 1500 and more inmates. Some respondents worked full time in facilities with fewer than 500 inmates. This factor alone adds elements of confusion and subjectivity to the presumption that size might have something to do with the amount of time spent or the work done by chaplains within that facility. It seems to indicate the lack of any basic central game plan on the part of the State's

Department of Corrections with regards to chaplains, and muddles even more the question of what the state expects of chaplaincy.

Moreover, judging by the comments made by chaplains, those who are working hard and who are devoted to their task would surely welcome clarity of expectations and close scrutiny if it would free them of chaplains within the system who give chaplaincy a bad name. From the observations made by chaplains about other chaplains, they see scattered answerablility as to the number of hours for which chaplains are hired (and paid) and the hours which they work, and for the basic attitudes of some chaplains. "I believe that the prison chaplaincy is a great work, and could be much greater, but you have some chaplains that are totally unworthy to be chaplains," complained one respondent. "They are only in it for the money and they really don't have any real concerns for the inmates. Some of them are more correctional officers than they are chaplains, and this type of chaplain really hurts the true, sincere chaplain's work" (47).

Another added: "One thing that I see as a problem area is general accountability of the chaplains. Many work hard and faithfully. Some do not" (15).

The criminal justice system is woefully compartmentalized and bureaucratized in any event. Confusion often reigns as to separate and conflicting policies issued at different levels of administration, all of which are to be carried out on a front line in facilities by officers and staff members who have little or no input in decisonmaking. For the sake of all who work in facilities, representative councils — even if they are only advisory — should be created which bring together these separated levels of decisionmakers and personnel. Such councils would be highly beneficial to chaplains. Mutual expectations could be clarified, the role of chaplains could be defined, shaped by the needs of individual facilities, and the issue of accountability would be brought into focus.

When asked to whom they turn to find out when they are doing a good job, the majority of chaplains answering the questionnaire had said, "I ask the inmates." Following the lead of these chaplains, it might be suggested that representative inmates sit on such councils. Those who might balk at this are to be reminded that, when prison riots occur and hostages are taken, the powers that be take hat in hand and listen to inmate grievances and demands. Why wait until another uprising? Inmates should be chosen who have the respect of their peers, as well as the respect of officers and staff. Their input about what is needed within facilities should be heard. They should help to define the role of chaplains, and at least some portion of each chaplain's accountability should be a matter of their scrutiny.

SUGGESTIONS FOR FUTURE STUDIES IN CRIMINAL JUSTICE

If one agrees with the findings of Daniel Glaser (1964) that, while chaplains constitute only a fraction of the total prison staff, they have an effect upon inmates which is greatly disproportionate to their numbers, then it is amazing that almost nothing has been written about them in the field of criminal justice. This study, allowing chaplains to speak for themselves about their role within the system, is seminal. It could be used as an instigation for further studies about dimensions and issues concerning this role.

One limitation of this present study has been that that those who returned the survey might justifiably be considered as nonrepresentative of the whole range of chaplains. One would want to see a future study done which manages to corral the chaplains about whom complaints were voiced by those chaplains who filled out the questionnaire — e.g., the "no shows," "minimal shows," the old man who comes in once a week to drink tea, and the clergy for whom chaplaincy means only a well paid sinecure. The chaplains who responded to the survey were more experienced in the number of years spent in chaplaincy than the general population of chaplains in the system. These respondents were men and women who evidently remained in chaplaincy after getting accustomed to it and deciding that it was meant for them. In contrast to them, one would like to hear from those chaplains who decided, after brief duration, that chaplaincy was not meant for them, or who could not take the pressures involved. As difficult as it would be to track these people down, their responses, in a future, more extensive study, might add an important dimension to a portrait of chaplaincy.

The chaplains who responded were preponderantly white males, representing the Catholic and Protestant faith groups. Given the small representation of women, black, Islamic, and Jewish chaplains, it would be unproductive to make assumptions about the effect of background differences on the experience of chaplains.

Such limitations leave areas unexplored which might warrant further study. A study, for example, focusing upon the difficulties and special needs of African American chaplains would be of great value. black inmates are the dominant population within the system. The system is administered overwhelmingly by whites. Moreover, for the span of several decades of time a strong, oftentimes hostile competition has been waged within black inmate populations as to whether the Islamic Faith is better representative of black culture than is Christianity. This competition creates tension situations which must be handled by both Islamic and Christian black chaplains. It is a dramatic story, yet to be told.

Feminist issues have touched almost every aspect of modern thinking, including the role of women within the criminal justice system. While the inmate population is predominantly male and chaplaincy is, proportionately, a male dominated profession, the role of females ministers within chaplaincy should be explored in itself. This would concern not only their effectiveness in ministering within women's facilities but in facilities for men as well. Sister Joan Campbell, whose own ministry bears witness to the strength that women can bring to this ministry, observes: "The gifts that are peculiar to womanhood-manhood, sexuality and sensuality, can have a profound impact on pastoral relationships and liturgy and can assist one's spiritual journey. While having an appropriate relationship with a chaplain or volunteer of the same sex is valuable, the added dimensions of an appropriate relationship with the opposite sex can be profound" (1989:34).

Other issues touched upon in this study could be explored more extensively. Official chaplains reacted strongly to the confusion which can be created by volunteer groups wishing to invade and "save souls" within prisons. In the current age of populist, televangelist, "instant solution religion," this problem is persistent and multi faceted. The issue is worthy of a detailed study of its own, for it can well be argued that such high powered, emotionally intense expressions of religion would be preferred by many inmates over main line denominations. The great question to be focused upon is whether facilities — already uncomfortable with the presence of main line denominations — could withstand the pressures of pros-eyletizing on the tiers and the unleashing of the emotions — both positive and negative — which would be involved.

"There is a great feeling of being needed; I have a wonderful ministry to inmates with AIDS," (28) wrote the priest at a large maximum security prison. The issue of AIDS as a personal stress factor was written off as insignificant by the respondents. And yet, at this writing, AIDS is intruding ever more insistently into the American consciousness, and, if no cure is found, will become a far more pressing concern in the future. This is especially so in facilities where inmate populations, owing to various life styles, are highly at risk as a group. It might happen that in a few short years many prisons will have become hospices for the dying. Such a situation would have a profound impact upon the role of the chaplain. Some facilities, such as Comstock, have already had to deal with growing dormitories of AIDS patients/inmates, and much of the pain of dealing with this has to fall to the chaplains. It will be a special ministry of itself and will need much education and study. Despite the limitations of the present study, however, the revelations made by the responding chaplains about chaplaincy itself, helps to fill a great gap of knowledge in an aspect of prison life about which almost nothing has been written. The picture created is not complete, but it is a beginning.

A MESSAGE TO THE VARIOUS FAITH COMMUNITIES

"A church that is interested in prisoners doesn't have to look far," notes Duane Pederson, observing, "Every community has at least a jail." For this reason, he judges: "It is this nearness that is also part of the shameful neglect by churches for prison ministries. Between 1,500 and 2000 jails have no religious services for inmates."

The major faith groups and mainline denominations would do well hear to the criticisms set forth by a number of well-meaning people throughout this study, individuals such as Sing Sing's articulate warden Lewis Lawes who told churches to stop issuing pious platitudes and to give evidence, instead, of real interest in rehabilitating lives. They should listen to the lifers at Angola prison whose newsletter heaps scorn upon the mainline religions for cutting off those who are incarcerated as if they no longer existed.

There is no special calling to minister to the men and women who are sentenced to live in cages in our country. God demands it of all who would say that they believe in God. If individual members of faith groups cannot stomach going into these cages, they must, nonetheless, see to it that there are members of their faith group who can stomach it and will enter them. They simply cannot, as a faith group, turn their backs upon the situation and pretend that these people do not exist. God demands that they address themselves to it. Those who do enter these cages should receive ongoing spiritual, physical and emotional support from those who share Faith with them. Clergy ministering to congregations should visit the imprisoned from their congregations as routinely as they would visit those who are in hospitals. Rather than the "either-or" division of ministerial realms, clergy serving in outside congregations might well might extend the practice of "pulpit sharing" by volunteering to join chaplains of their own denominations in occasional religious services at a facility. This would reduce the chasm which exists in the minds of religious-minded members of congregations who indulge in the luxury of separating their own lives from the lives of those who are incarcerated, for their own pastor will have become an example of healing and rehabilitating.

It would reduce the feeling, experienced by many chaplains, that their ministry is not understood or appreciated by others of their own Faith. Those who serve as official chaplains frequently point out their own haphazard assignment into this ministry, and that they entered into it with trepidation — "I came with great fear . . . " (22). Others regret the lack of any kind of training, saying that "chaplaincy should be better explained to candidates for the job" (35). "I entered it knowing nothing about it," said one, "I was put into it with no special training or orientation" (20). "Many chaplains are not well prepared for this work," concluded another, adding, "The Church should establish a national institute for the training — initial and ongoing — of chaplains. The Church should train, not the state" (60).

These attestations should be a call to a greater sense of ecclesiastical professionalism in this field. Regional communities of faith groups should establish ongoing liasons with the national Prison Chaplains associations. They should take the initiative in offering seminars and workshops for students of theology. Perhaps teams of chaplains should be regularly invited to visit seminaries and schools of theology to interest and educate potential newcomers into chaplaincy as to the realities of this ministry. faith groups should work with chaplains associations on a national level to increase public relations efforts to educate outsiders as to the importance of ministry to the incarcerated. Not only should clergy be trained, but laypersons as well. Those interested in volunteering to work with the incarcerated (e.g., in educational programs, family outreach programs) should be given both encouragement and proper training in ongoing regional workshops and support groups.

THE CALLING

What comes through in this study of chaplains is a realization that there is a quiet sense of the heroic in what these men and women accomplish out of love for God and humanity. Their lives are hidden from public view; one does not see testimonial banquets as chaplains mark milestone years in their work. These ministers freely choose to remain where they are, "in spite of overwhelming injustices and the negativity of the environment," (4) so that they might "bring God's love to people in a very harsh setting" (2). What they give witness to makes one, in a humble sense, proud to be of their number. Their authentic and honest words about ministry remind one of school posters, in a former age, pushing students toward the heroism of religious life when such a commitment was seen, not as being of advantage to those who might enter this life, but as advantageous for others.

The call remains that of Matthew XXV — "I was in prison and you visited me, for whatever you did for the least of these, you did for me." It is a call which clearly transcends any one faith group. It is a reminder that, even without a clear definition of role, chaplains must be "a humane influence in a very brutal system" (49). Ultimately, it is not the system which matters, but those who are within it. As one chaplain wrote: "I perceive the incarcerated as being among the poorest of the poor (to quote Mother Teresa) who need help (i.e., our presence, our support) more than others" (20).

It should be a matter of top priority to the leaders of various faith groups that they focus attention upon the significant contributions of the men and women who serve in this hidden ministry. Official recognition of their work should emphasize that chaplaincy within penal institutions is not tangent, but rather, central to the universal ministry of all faith groups. Such recognition would also serve as a public proclamation affirming that the rehabilitation of criminal offenders is essential to the purposes of organized religions.

Religious authorities should actively recruit among clergy to fill the ranks of chaplains, and such recruitment should be an appeal made to those who might wish to make a difference in coping with the worst of society's problems. If formal training institutes are established for those who are entering a ministry to the incarcerated, those who would set up a curriculum for such institutes would do well to use as a basic text the philosophy and practical advice offered in the words of all these dedicated chaplains who have been tempered by experience in this field.

NOTES

1. Federal chaplains, working in regionalized facilities throughout the United States, disregarded this issue, ranking it near the bottom of the list of stress factors both in occurrence (mean 1.9) and in intensity of demand (mean 1.7) Chaplains working in State prisons, and especially those ministering in County jails, are likely to be recruited from nearby communities of their congregations. This issue showed itself to be something of a "wild card." While the majority of these chaplains (55.7%) ranked the issue of carrying on a "simultaneous ministry to inmates and to a congregation outside the facility" 1-2 on the frequency scale, 17.1% rated it as a 5 (constant factor). The scale measuring intensity of the demand showed negligible discomfort (mean 2.1), with 65.7% rating the conflict 1-2. The only significant difference which emerged in the T-test scores was a plausible one, involving chaplains with different combinations of assignments. But this difference lay between those chaplains working 21-80% and those working over 80% of their schedule within a facility. The 2-tail probability score was .035. Only nine of the chaplains worked less than 20%, yet two of these rated the inside/outside issue a 5 both in prevalence and discomfort. Of the 20 chaplains working 21-79% of their schedule in a facility, six rated the conflict a 5 in frequency and three a 5 in intensity. Of the 37 chaplains who worked over 80% of their schedule inside a facility, only four rated the problem a 5 in prevalence and none of these rated it a 5 in distress. Further, while there is an even spread of the 20-79% group in rating the item 1-5 in frequency, 59% of the chaplains working over 80% wrote off the problem, rating it a 1-2 in occurrence, and 67.5% assigned it a low score (1-2) on the discomfort scale.

2. While this writer/chaplain has always found the noise level on the tiers to be a great annoyance (I would rate it a 4 both in frequency and in intensity of discomfort) the item shows the importance of surveying the opinions of others; neither the State nor Federal chaplains ranked it high in the list of stress factors. In the first survey, New York State chaplains ranked it with a 3.0 mean in frequency and a 2.7 mean in discomfort. The Federal chaplains followed suit, ranking the noise factor within facilities a 2.7 mean in frequency and a 2.5 mean in discomfort.

REFERENCES

Abbott, Jack Henry (1981) *In the Belly of the Beast*. New York: Random House.

Ayers, Edward L. (1984) *Vengeance and Justice: Crime and Punishment in the Nineteenth Century American South*. New York: Oxford University Press.

Ballesteros, Octavio A. (1979) *Behind Jail Bars*. New York: Philisophical Library.

Barnes, Harry Elmer (1968) *The Evolution of Penology in Pennsylvania*. Montclair, NJ: Patterson Smith.

Bartollas, Clemens, Stuart J. Miller, and Simon Dinitz (1976) *Juvenile Victimization: The Institutional Paradox*. New York: Sage.

Bartollas, Clemens, and Stuart J. Miller (1978) *The Juvenile Offender: Control, Correction and Treatment*. Boston: Allyn and Bacon.

Bates, Sanford (1936) *Prisons and Beyond* New York: MacMillan.

Benney, Mark (1948) *Gaol Delivery*. London: Longman's, Green.

Berkmans, Ronald (1979) *Opening the Gates: The Rise of the Prisoner's Movement*. Lexington, MA: Lexington Books.

Berrigan, Philip (1970) *Prison Journals of a Priest Revolutionary*. New York: Holt, Rinehart and Winston.

Bok, Curtis (1959) *Star Wormwood*. New York: Alfred A. Knopf.

Butler, Keith (1978) "The Muslims Are No Longer an Unknown Quantity," *Corrections Magazine*, 4 (July): 56-59.

Butts, W. Marlin (1966) "The Role of Religion and the Church in Corrections." *Proceedings of the Eleventh Annual Southern Conference on Corrections* Tallahassee, FL: Florida State University.

Campbell, Joan (1989) *The Ministry to the Imprisoned*. Collegeville, MN: Liturgical Press.

Camelli, Louis John (September 1979) "The Response of Spirituality," *Chicago Studies*, V. 18 n. 1. Pp 97-109.

Charriere, Henri (1970) *Papillon*. New York: William Morrow.

Cheek, Frances E., and Maria DiStefano Miller, (1979) *The Experience of Stress For Corrections Officers*. Cincinnati: Paper presented at the American Academy of Criminal Justice Sciences.

Clay, John, Rev. (1861) *The Prison Chaplain*. Montclair, NJ: Patterson Smith.

Clemmer, Donald (1958) *The Prison Community*. New York: Holt, Rinehart and Winston.

Cole, Larry (1972) *Our Children's Keepers*. New York: Grossman.

Corey, Bruce (1979) "Texas v. Brother Roloff," *Corrections Magazine*. 5 (September) 20 - 24.

Cottle, Charles R. (1968) *Sunrise*. Fort Madison, IA: Dodd.

De Beaumont, Gustave, and Alexis de Tocqueville (1964) *On the Penitentiary System in the United States and Its Application in France.* Carbondale, IL: Southern Illinois University Press.

Eriksson, Torsten (1976) *The Reformers.* New York: Elsevier.

Fenton, Norman (1973) *Human Relations in Adult Corrections.* Springfield, IL: Charles C. Thomas.

Finley, James B. (1974) *Memorials of Prison Life.* New York: Arno.

Fitzharris, Timothy (1973) *The Desirability of a Correctional Ombudsman.* Berkely, CA: Institute of Governmental Studies, University of California.

Fogel, David (1975) *We Are the Living Proof: The Justice Model of Corrections.* Cincinnati: Anderson.

Fox, Lionel W. (1952) *The English Prison and Borstal Systems.* London: Routledge and Kegan Paul.

Freudenberger, H.J., and Richelson, G. (1980) *Burnout; The High Cost of High Achievement.* Garden City: Anchor.

Gage, Freddie (1986) *All My Friends are Dead.* Dallas: International Prison Ministry.

Glaser, Daniel (1964) *The Effectiveness of a Prison and Parole System.* Indianapolis: Bobbs-Merrill.

Gleuck, Sheldon (1959) *The Problem of Delinquency.* Boston: Houghton Mifflin.

Godwin, John (1963) *Alcatraz: 1868-1963.* Garden City: Doubleday.

Griswold, Jack, Mike Misenheimer, Art Powers, and Ed Tromanhauser. (1970) *An Eye for an Eye.* New York: Holt, Rinehart and Winston.

Grunhut, Max (1972) *Penal Reform.* Montclair, NJ: Patterson Smith.

Handlin, Oscar (1977) *Boston's Immigrants.* New York: Atheneum.

Heffernan, Esther (1972) *Making It In Prison: The Square, the Cool, and the Life.* New York: Wiley-Interscience.

Henderson, Charles R. (1910) *Prison Reform.* New York: New York Charities Publication Committee.

Irwin, John (1985) *The Jail.* Berkeley: University of California Press.

Jackson, Bruce, and Diane Christian (1980) *Death Row.* Boston: Beacon Press.

Jacobs, James B. (1977) *Stateville: The Penitentiary in Mass Society.* Chicago: Universtiy of Chicago Press.

Jacobs, James B., and Harold G. Retsky (1975) "Prison Guard," *Urban Life* 4,1 (April):5-29.

Janson, Frances O. (1978) *Management and Supervision of Small Jails.* Springfield, IL: Charles C. Thomas.

Johnson, Elmer H. (1968) *Crime, Correction and Society,* 2d ed. Homewood, IL: Dorsey.

Johnson, Elmer H. (1974) *Crime, Correction and Society,* 3rd ed. Homewood, IL: Dorsey.

Johnson, Elmer H. (1978) *Crime, Correction and Society*, 4th ed. Homewood, IL: Dorsey.

Johnson, Robert (1977) "Ameliorating Prison Stress: Some Helping Roles for Custodial Personnel," *International Journal of Crime and Penology*. 5:263-273.

Johnson, Robert (1981) *Condemned to Die: Life Under the Sentence of Death*. New York: Elsevier.

Johnson, Robert, and Shelley Price (1981) "The Complete Correctional Officer: Human Services and the Human Environment of Prison," *Criminal Justice and Behavior* 8,3 (September):343-373.

Kalinich, David, and Frederick J. Postill (1981) *Principles of County Jail Administration*. Springfield, IL: Charles C. Thomas.

Kassebaum, Gene, David Warner and Daniel Wilner (1971) *Prison Treatment and Parole Survival: An Empirical Assessment*. New York: John Wiley.

Kelley, Joanna (1967) *When the Gates Shut*. London:Longman's, Green.

Keve, Paul W. (1984) *The McNeil Century: The Life and Times of an Island Prison*. Chicago: Nelson Hall.

Klare, Hugh J. (1960) *Anatomy of a Prison*. London: Hutchinson.

Klofas, John, and Hans Toch (1982) "The Guard Subculture Myth," *Journal of Research in Crime and Delinquency*. 19,2 (July):238- 254.

Lamott, Kenneth (1961) *Chronicles of San Quentin*. New York: David McKay.

Lawes, Lewis E. (1938) *Invisible Stripes*. New York: Farrar and Rinehart.

Lazarus, Richard S. (1966) *Psychological Stress and the Coping Factor*. New York: McGraw Hill.

Leffler, William J. (1973) "On Being Human in the Prison Community," *Behavioral Science and Modern Penology* (Ed. William H. Lyle, Jr. and Thetus W. Homer) Springfield, IL: Charles C. Thomas.

Leibert, Julius A., with Emily Kingsberg (1965) *Behind Bars: What a Chaplain Saw in Alcatraz, Folsom and San Quentin*. Garden City: Doubleday.

Lombardo, Lucien X. (1981) "Occupational Stress in Corrections Officers: Sources, Coping, Strategies and Implications," *Corrections at the Crossroads: Designing Policy*. (Ed. Sherwood E. Zimmerman and Harold D. Miller) Beverly Hills: Sage.

Maslach, Christina, (1981) *Burnout: - The Cost of Caring*. Englewood Cliffs, NJ: Prentice Hall.

MacDonald, A.R. (1893) *Prison Secrets: Things Seen, Suffered, and Recorded During Seven Years in Ludlow Street Jail*. New York: Acme.

Mattick, Hans W., and Ronald P. Sweet (1970) *Illinois Jails: Challenge and Opportunity for the 1970s*. Chicago: Illinois Law Enforcement Commission.

McGrath, Joseph E. (1970) *Social and Psychological Factors in Stress*. New York; Holt, Rinehart and Winston.

McKelvey, Blake (1977) *American Prisons: A History of Good Intentions*. Montclair, NJ: Patterson Smith.

Mechanic, David, (1962) *Students Under Stress*. Madison: University of Wisconson Press.

Metts, James R., and Thomas Cook. (1982) "Full Service Chaplaincy Program," *Innovations in South Carolina Law Enforcement* (Ed. Patricia Walter). Columbia, SC: Division of Public Safety, Office of the Governor. Pp. 23-33.

Moore, Daniel G. (1969) *Enter Without Knocking*. Tucson: University of Arizona Press.

Munro, John Josiah (1909) *The New York Tombs Inside and Out* Brooklyn: Published by Author.

Murphy, George L. (1956) *The Social Role of the Prison Chaplain*. Doctoral Dissertation, University of Pittsburgh.

Nelson, Victor F. (1933) *Prison Days and Nights*. Boston: Little, Brown.

Olsson, Barbara H., and Ann Dargis (1981) "Occupational Stress in Correction Officers — Sources, Coping Strategies, and Implications," *Corrections at the Crossroads* (Eds. Sherwood .E Zimmerman and Harold D. Miller.) Beverly Hills: Sage. Pp 129- 149.

Pederson, Duane. (1979) *How to Establish a Jail and Prison Ministry*. Nashville: Thomas Nelson.

Playfair, Giles (1971) *The Punitive Obsession*. London: Victor Gollaney.

Poole, Eric D., and Robert M. Regoli (1980) "Role Stress, Custody Orientation and Disciplinary Actions — A Study of Prison Guards," *Criminology* (August) 18(2), 215 -226.

Post, James E. (1968) "The Role of the Chaplain," *Eighth Annual Corrections Officers Seminar: A Report*. Kansas: University of Kansas. Pp. 95-96.

Potter, Joan (1978) "In Prison, Women Are Different," *Corrections Magazine,* December, 4(6), 21-29.

Powers, George E. (1967) "Prevention Through Religion," *Delinquency Prevention*. (Ed. William E. Amos and Charles Wellford) Englewood Cliffs, NJ: Prentice Hall. Pp 99-127.

President's Commission on Law Enforcement and the Administration of Justice (1967) *Task Force Report: Organized Crime*. Washington, DC: U.S. Government Printing Office.

Priestley, Philip (1980) *Community of Scapegoats: The Segregation of Sex Offenders and Informers in Prison*. Oxford: Pergamon.

Ragen, Joseph, and Charles Finston (1962) *Inside the World's Toughest Prison*. Springfield, IL: Charles C. Thomas.

Reynolds, John (1834) *Recollections of Windsor Prison*. Boston: A. Wright.

Rideau, W., and B. Sinclair (1981) "Religion in Prison," *Angolite*. (January) Pp. 31- 56.

Roberts, Albert (1971) *Sourcebook on Prison Education*. Springfield, IL: Charles C. Thomas.

Runyan, Tom (1953) *In For Life*. New York: W.W. Norton.

Ryan, Patrick J. (September 12, 1992) "Astuteness," *America*, September 12, 167:6, p. 151.

Selye, Hans. (1956) *The Stress of Life*. New York: McGraw Hill.

Scudder, Kenyon J. (1952) *Prisoners are People*. Garden City: Doubleday.

Shaw, Richard (1976) *Dagger John*. New York: Paulist Press.

Smith, Ann D. (1962) *Women in Prison: A Study in Penal Methods*. London: Stevens.

Stolz, Barbara Ann (1978) *Prisons as Political Institutions — What Are the Implications for Prison Ministry?* College Park: American Correctional Association.

Taft, Philip B. Jr. (1978) "Whatever Happened to That Old Time Prison Chaplain?" *Corrections Magazine* (December) 4(4), 54-61.

Taft, Philip B. Jr. (1979) "Religious Reformers Want to Proclaim Liberty to the Captives," *Corrections Magazine* (December) 5 (4), 37- 43.

Task Force Report: Corrections. (1967) *United States President's Commission on Law Enforcement and Administration of Justice*. Washington: U.S. Government Printing Office.

Teeters, Negley K. (1955) *The Cradle of the Penitentiary (The Walnut Street Jail at Philadelphia)*. Philadelphia: Temple University Press.

Teeters, Negley K, and John D. Shearer (1957) *The Prison at Philadelphia: Cherry Hill*. New York: Columbia University Press.

Toch, Hans, and J. Douglas Grant (1982) *Performing Human Services: Change Through Participation*. Beverly Hills: Sage.

Toch, Hans, and John Klofas (1982) "Alienation and Desire for Job Enrichment Among Correction Officers," *Federal Probation*, March, 46:1, 35-44.

Veninga, Robert L., and Spradley, James P. (1981) *The Work Stress Connection; How to Cope With Job Burnout*. Boston: Little, Brown.

W.B.N. (1903) *Penal Servitude*. New York. G.P. Putnam's Sons.

Walrod, Truman, (Ed.) (1970) *Manual on Jail Administration*. Washington, D.C.: National Sheriffs Association.

Ward, Harry (1972) "The Contribution of Religion to the Criminal Justice System." *Seventh Annual Conference on Corrections* (Ed. Vernon Fox). Tallahasee: Florida State University Press. Pp. 124- 129.

Weir, Eligius, and Leo Kalm (1936) *Crime and Religion: A Study of Criminological Facts and Problems*. Chicago: Franciscan Herald Press.

Weiss, Karl (Ed.) (1976) *The Prison Experience*. New York: Delacorte.

Wickman, Peter (1983) "Role Conflict and Stress of Prison Guards: Organizational and Cross National Perspectives," *Comparative Criminology*, (Ed. Israel Barak-Glantz) Beverly Hills: Sage.

Willet, T.S. (1983) "Prison Guards in Private," *Canadian Journal of Criminology*. (January) 25, 1 -17.

Williams, J.E. Hall (1975) *Changing Prisons*. London: Peter Owen.

Wines, Frederick H. (1919) *Punishment and Reformation*. New York: Thomas Crowell.

Wolff, Michael (1967) *Prison*. London: Eyre and Spottiswoods.

Zimbardo, Philip G. (1975) *Prison Behavior*. Springfield, VA: Office of Naval Research.

APPENDICES

I: PRISON/JAIL CHAPLAINCY QUESTIONNAIRE

What satisfaction do you find in ministry to the incarcerated that makes it unique compared to other areas of ministry?

If you wrote a job description of Jail/Prison ministry, what would you include?

Stress does not mean that we cannot cope with our environment. Stress occurs when we feel an imbalance between the demands placed on us and the resources we have for meeting them. Taxing situations of this kind would be labelled stress factors. Scale the following demands of ministering in a facility according to the frequency of the demand (Column A) and its intensity (Column B). Circle one in Column A and one in Column B.

- *Column A contained a five point scale for frequency of demand, with the following anchor-definitions: 1 = Never   3 = Occasional   5 = Constant*
- *Column B contained a six-point scale for intensity of demand, with the following anchor-definitions: 1 = Not at all   3 = Moderate   5 = Significant*

☐ The noise factor within facilities (e.g. constant yelling, TVs, etc.)
☐ The potential for physical danger
☐ The possibility of contracting an illness such as AIDS or Hepatitis
☐ Invasion of inmate privacy when working on the tiers (toilets areas etc.)
☐ The sense of invading privacy when working on tiers of the opposite sex
☐ Preaching about a loving God within a punishment setting
☐ Overcrowding, and the subsequent overloading of ministerial responsibilities
☐ Unruly behavior at Religious services (using services as a social gathering, etc.)
☐ Being subject to two chains of command — civil as well as religious
☐ Bureaucratic paper work required by the facility
☐ Frustration about observed injustices within the Criminal Justice System
☐ Simultaneous ministry to inmates and to a congregation outside the facility
☐ Dealing with simplistic public attitudes about offenders
☐ Working in a hidden ministry isolated from fellow clergy

Of the items which you checked, do any one or two of them stand out as being personally, very demanding?

Feel free to clarify or expand upon any of the above or to mention any other demands of this ministry.

Chaplains have accepted the task of serving others in a setting wherein many pressures affect relationships. Please evaluate the following demands placed on relationships. Please scale the following demands on relationships in the same manner as above, first as to the frequency of the demands in Column A, and the intensity of such in Column B. (Again, circle one in Column A and one in Column B).

- *Again, Column A contained a five point scale for frequency of demand, with the following anchor-definitions: 1 = Never   3 = Occasional   5 = Constant*
- *Column B contained a six-point scale for intensity of demand, with the following anchor-definitions: 1 = Not at all   3 = Moderate   5 = Significant*

☐ The social chasm which exists between most chaplains and inmates

☐ Discovering that a trusted inmate has conned you for his/her own purposes

☐ The infrequency of success stories in the after release lives of presumably rehabilitated inmates

☐ Hearing the same stories over and over, told by inmates who fit very predictable patterns of behavior

☐ Dealing with inmates' family crises when it is beyond your means to alleviate the situation (e.g., by obtaining a furlough, etc.)

☐ Being unable to emotionally draw back from the unrelieved problems of inmates

☐ Having to balance non-judgmental sympathy with the preaching of morality

☐ Reacting emotionally against the dislikable personalities of some inmates

☐ Dealing with mentally ill inmates who should be in hospitals rather than in prisons

☐ Being burdened with confidences which should be known by authorities

☐ Living in a prison reality where mores are dictated by inmate codes

☐ Racial/religious tensions

☐ Dealing with volunteer groups and activists who fail to understand the special security needs of facilities

☐ Conflict with Corrections Officers and other facility staff members

☐ Frictions which arise between chaplains (or volunteer religious groups) of different denominations or even within the same denomination

Of the items which you checked do any one or two items stand out as being personally, very demanding?

Feel free to expand upon any of the above points or include any other factors involving human relations within a facility which might create a demand upon one's ministry.

COPING WITH THE DEMANDS OF MINISTRY

If someone were to ask you *As a chaplain, how do you know when you are doing a good job?*, what would you say?

Do you have any special decompression techniques which help you to leave the facility behind you emotionally when you leave it for the day?

Spiritual writers speak of the idea of Kenosis — that the person of God is one whose life is poured out for others. And yet, we must balance the demands of this life-for-others with common sense precautions for the sake of physical and emotional well-being. If you were to educate a newcomer to this ministry as to how to alleviate the demands of this work, what precautions, or activities, etc., would you suggest to him or her?

To whom do you turn for spiritual and professional direction in dealing with your ministry?

Is your thinking, or philosoph, about jail/prison ministry different now than at the onset of you work within a facility? If so, how?

Do you see yourself in this ministry five years from now?

Please feel free to include any alternate perspective about chaplaincy or to expand upon any of the concerns touched upon in this questionnaire.

BACKGROUND QUESTIONS

Please circle the type of facility wherein your ministry is exercised:

County Jail	*Facility for men*	*Minimun security*
State Prison	*Facility for women*	*Medium security*
Federal Prison	*Facility for both*	*Maximum security*

What is the size of the facility (i.e., number of inmates)?

Is the facility situated in a large metropolitan area, medium sized city, small town, or rural area?

How many years have you served in Jail/Prison ministry?

How many years have you been in ministry altogether?

What ministerial responsibilities do you have outside of your Jail/Prison ministry?

What percentage of you ministerial time is spent in Jail/Prison ministry?

Please supply the following data:

Age/years
Sex
Marital status
Religious Affiliation
Race and/or Ethnic background

IF YOU WOULD BE INTERESTED IN RECEIVING A COPY OF THE RESULTS OF THIS STUDY JUST DROP ME A POSTCARD WITH YOUR ADDRESS ON IT AND I WILL BE HAPPY TO SEND IT TO YOU. AGAIN, THANKS FOR YOUR HELP.

II: LETTER OF INVITATION TO PARTICIPATE

Dear Chaplain:

I am a chaplain serving at the Summit Shock Incarceration Facility and Albany County Jail and have served in ministry to the incarcerated since 1972. The enclosed questionnaire about the Prison/jail ministry not only incorporates longstanding concerns of mine but would enable me to document a dissertation I am writing, one of the requirements of a degree in Criminal Justice at the State University of New York at Albany.

Dr. Hans Selye, who pioneered in medical understanding of stress, noted that pressures which enter our lives "cause wear and tear, making demands for adaptation." Cary Cherniss, a psychologist at Rutgers University, writing about job stress in human services, observed that "stress occurs when there is a perceived imbalance between resources and demands." Those of us who minister to the incarcerated do so with extraordinary demands placed upon us. And yet, it is a challenge which we willingly accept.

The benefits of this study would be to help us evaluate these demands on us which can cause stress, and, more importantly, to share means of coping with these stress factors. Thus, input from you by sharing your ideas in this questionnaire would be an invaluable help and contribution to our vocation.

In order to respect privacy and a preference for anonymity, the questionnaire need not be signed. If, however, you would be interested in seeing the results of the survey, just send the enclosed postcard with your return address listed, and I'll be happy to share these responses with you.

If there are any areas of concern which you think are not covered by the questionnaire please feel free to add them.

I greatly appreciate your assistance.

Fraternally,

Rev. Richard Shaw
St. Gabriel's Church
3040 Hamburg St.
Schenectady, N.Y. 12303

III: CODED ROSTER OF CHAPLAIN RESPONDENTS

The assigned numbers correspond to the quotes in the text. The data, as listed in order after each number, indicates the government level and the security level of the facility, and whether it is a facility for men women, or both. The personal characteristics as listed, in order, indicate the Faith group, race, sex, and years in chaplaincy for each respondent.

- *1. State, medium, men; Catholic, White, male, 13.*
- *2. State, medium, women; Protestant, Black, female, 5.*
- *3. State, minimum, men; Protestant, White, male, 13.*
- *4. State, medium, men; Protestant, White, female, 7.*
- *5. State, medium, men; Protestant, White, male, 5.*
- *6. State, medium, men; Protestant, Black, male, 2.*
- *7. State, medium, men; Protestant, White, male, 7.*
- *8. State, medium, men; Protestant, White, male, 10.*
- *10. State, maximum, men; Protestant, Black, male, 12.*
- *11. State, minimum, men; Protestant, White, male, 5.*
- *12. State, maximum, men; Protestant, White, male, 9.*
- *13. State, medium, men; Protestant, White, male, 2.*
- *14. State, medium, men; Protestant, White, male, 1.*
- *15. State, medium, men; Protestant, White, male, 5.*
- *16. State, medium, men; Catholic, White, male, 6.*
- *17. State, medium, men; Catholic, White, male, 1.*
- *18. State, medium, men; Catholic, White, male, 23.*
- *19. State, maximum, women; Catholic, White, male, 8.*
- *20. State, minimum, men; Catholic, White, male, 7.*
- *21. State, maximum, men; Catholic, White, female, 1.*
- *22. State, maximum, men; Catholic, White, male, 3.*
- *23. State, medium, men; Catholic, White, male, 11.*
- *24. State, maximum, men; Catholic, White, male, 10.*
- *25. State, medium, both; Catholic, White, male, 9.*
- *26. State, medium, men; Catholic, White, male, 23.*
- *27. State, maximum, men; Catholic, White, male, 14.*
- *28. State, maximum, men; Catholic, White, male, 11.*
- *29. State, maximum, men; Catholic, White, male, 10.*
- *30. State, maximum, men; Catholic, White, male, 5.*
- *31. State, medium, men; Catholic, White, male, 5.*
- *32. State, maximum, men; Catholic, White, male, 13.*
- *33. State, medium, men; Catholic, White, male, 7.*
- *34. State, maximum, men; Catholic, White, male, 3.*
- *35. State, medium, men; Catholic, White, male, 2.*
- *36. State, maximum, men; Catholic, White, male, 6.*
- *37. State, minimum, men; Catholic, White, male, 3.*

- *38. State, maximum, men; Catholic, White, male, 28.*
- *39. Federal, medium, men; Protestant, White, male, 18.*
- *40. Federal, minimum, men; Protestant, White, female, 10.*
- *41. Federal, medium, men; Protestant, White, female, 11.*
- *42. Federal, medium, men; Catholic, White, male, 12.*
- *43. Federal, maximum, men; Islamic, Black, male, 5.*
- *44. State, medium, men; Catholic, White, male, 4.*
- *45. State, maximum, men; Catholic, White, male, 1.*
- *46. State, maximum, men; Catholic, White, male, 3.*
- *47. State, maximum, both; Islamic, Black, male, 13.*
- *48. State, maximum, men; Islamic, Black, male, 5.*
- *49. State, Minimum, men; Catholic, White, male, 4.*
- *50. State, medium, men; Jewish, White, male, 31.*
- *51. State, medium, men; Jewish, White, male, 32.*
- *52. State, maximum, men; Jewish, White, male, 30.*
- *53. State, medium, men; Jewish, White, male, 2.*
- *54. State, medium, men; Jewish, White, male, 4.*
- *55. Metropolitan jail, maximum, men; Catholic, White, male, 2.*
- *56. Metropolitan jail, maximum, men; Jewish, White, male, 4.*
- *57. Metropolitan jail, maximum, both; Jewish, White, male, 6.*
- *58. Metropolitan jail, maximum, men; Jewish, White, male, 20.*
- *59. Metropolitan Jail, maximum, both; Protestant, White, male, 3.*
- *60. Metropolitan Jail, maximum, men; Catholic, White, male, 11.*
- *61. Metropolitan Jail, maximum, men; Catholic, White, male, 10.*
- *62. Metropolitan Jail, maximum, men; Catholic, White, male, 7.*
- *63. County Jail, maximum, both; Catholic, White, male, 2.*
- *64. County Jail, maximum, both; Catholic, White, male, 9.*
- *65. Metropolitan Jail, maximum, men; Catholic, White, male, 3.*
- *66. County Jail, maximum, both; Catholic, White, female, 15.*
- *67. Metropolitan Jail, maximum, men; Catholic, White, male, 3.*
- *68. County Jail, maximum, both; Catholic, White, female, 13.*
- *69. County Jail, maximum, both; Catholic, White, female, 13.*
- *70. Federal, minimum, male; Catholic, White, male, 17.*
- *71. Federal, minimum, male; Protestant, White, male, 12.*

Index of Names and Topics